OUR HEAVENLY SHEPHERD

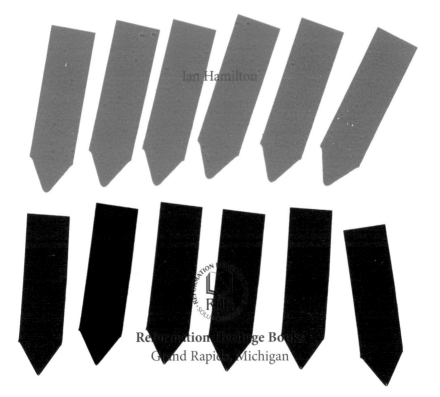

OUR HEAVENLY SHEPHERD
Comfort and Strength from Psalm 23

Ian Hamilton

Reformation Heritage Books
Grand Rapids, Michigan

Our Heavenly Shepherd
© 2022 by Ian Hamilton

Reformation Heritage Books
3070 29th St. SE, Grand Rapids, MI 49512
616-977-0889
orders@heritagebooks.org
www.heritagebooks.org

Printed in the United States of America
22 23 24 25 26 27/10 9 8 7 6 5 4 3 2 1

Library of Congress Cataloging-in-Publication Data

Names: Hamilton, Ian, author.
Title: Our heavenly shepherd : comfort and strength from Psalm 23 / Ian Hamilton.
Description: Grand Rapids, Michigan : Reformation Heritage Books, [2022] | Includes bibliographical references.
Identifiers: LCCN 2021042254 (print) | LCCN 2021042255 (ebook) | ISBN 9781601789143 (paperback) | ISBN 9781601789150 (epub)
Subjects: LCSH: Bible. Psalms, XXIII—Criticism, interpretation, etc.
Classification: LCC BS1450 23d .H335 2022 (print) | LCC BS1450 23d (ebook) | DDC 223/.206—dc23
LC record available at https://lccn.loc.gov/2021042254
LC ebook record available at https://lccn.loc.gov/2021042255

For additional Reformed literature, request a free book list from Reformation Heritage Books at the above regular or email address.

To my dear friends William and Margaret Dunlop, whose friendship over many years has been a constant encouragement to my wife and me.

Contents

Introduction

The book of Psalms comprises one hundred and fifty songs of worship compiled over approximately six hundred years. We do not know precisely when the final edition of the Psalms was compiled or who was responsible for the compilation. Over the past thirty years, studies in the nature, purpose, structure, and flow of the Psalms have become significant features of biblical studies.[1] The purpose of this brief exposition and reflection on Psalm 23, however, does nothing to advance the scholarly insights that have so enriched the study of the Psalms in recent years. Rather, this exposition seeks to unpack the theological and pastoral riches so eloquently set forth in this psalm.

During my twenty years as a parish minister in Loudoun Church of Scotland, Newmilns, I presided over seven hundred funerals. During at least half of these we sang the Twenty-Third Psalm, always to the Scottish tune Crimond. The reason for choosing this psalm so often was that it simply and beautifully set forth the Christian hope. The Lord

---

1. See O. Palmer Robertson, *The Flow of the Psalms* (Phillipsburg, N.J.: P&R Publishing, 2015).

God Almighty is the faithful heavenly Shepherd of His sheep, and He not only will faithfully lead His sheep in life but will accompany them as they walk through the valley of the shadow of death and will bring them into His house, where He will dwell with them forever.

The psalm is also a heart-searching challenge to unbelievers, especially religious unbelievers. King David's confidence as he faces the valley of the shadow of death and as he finds himself surrounded by enemies is not that he has been good and faithful (he hadn't been), or that he was a child of the covenant (which he was), but that the Lord Himself is with him: "You are with me." The true Christian's hope in life and in death is memorably expressed in the first question and answer of the Heidelberg Catechism:

Q: What is your only comfort in life and in death?

A: That I am not my own, but belong body and soul, in life and in death to my faithful Savior, Jesus Christ. He has fully paid for all my sins with his precious blood, and has set me free from the tyranny of the devil. He also watches over me in such a way that not a hair can fall from my head without the will of my Father in heaven; in fact, all things must work together for my salvation. Because I belong to him, Christ, by his Holy Spirit, assures me of eternal life and makes me wholeheartedly willing and ready from now on to live for him.

Best Known and Most Loved

Psalm 23 is probably the best known and most read passage in the Bible. It is a wonderfully reassuring picture of the believer's life. One of the psalm's most impressive and notable features is how often the personal, singular pronoun is used: "The LORD is my shepherd; I shall not want. He makes me... He leads me." God cares for His people not in the "lump," but individually and personally. It is true that the various pictures of the church in the New Testament are corporate pictures: the church is the body of Christ, the bride of Christ, the temple of God, the family of God. We read in Ephesians 5:25 that Christ loved the church and gave Himself for her. These vivid and evocative pictures of the church should not, however, detract from the personal commitment of God to individual believers. Paul could write that the Son of God "loved me and gave Himself for me" (Gal. 2:20). The heavenly Shepherd watches over, leads, provides for, and protects His sheep with a personalized, individual care and compassion. As our Lord Jesus impressed on His disciples, "the very hairs of your head are all numbered. Do not fear therefore" (Luke 12:7).

God the Shepherd

The depiction of the Lord as David's Shepherd is not unique to Psalm 23. The first reference to God as the Shepherd of His people is found in Genesis 49:24, where He is described as "the Mighty God of Jacob (from there is the Shepherd, the Stone of Israel)." Later in Israel's history, through His prophet Ezekiel, the Lord castigates the shepherds, the spiritual leaders, who had failed God's people so dismally (see Ezek. 34). In the midst of His searing condemnation of these false-hearted shepherds, the Lord declares, "'I will feed My flock, and I will make them lie down,' says the Lord GOD. 'I will seek what was lost and bring back what was driven away, bind up the broken and strengthen what was sick;

but I will destroy the fat and the strong, and feed them in judgment'" (Ezek. 34:15–16).

The picture of God as the Shepherd of His people is rich in its imagery. Shepherds were absolute "monarchs" of their sheepfolds. They held unquestioned authority over their sheep. They were the providers and protectors of their sheep. They alone were responsible for leading their sheep to green pastures and still waters and for protecting them from wild animals and marauding bandits. When David offered himself to King Saul to fight Goliath, the Philistine giant who was publicly mocking God, he said, "'Your servant used to keep his father's sheep, and when a lion or a bear came and took a lamb out of the flock, I went out after it and struck it, and delivered the lamb from its mouth; and when it arose against me, I caught it by its beard, and struck and killed it. Your servant has killed both lion and bear; and this uncircumcised Philistine will be like one of them, seeing he has defied the armies of the living God.' Moreover David said, 'The LORD, who delivered me from the paw of the lion and from the paw of the bear, He will deliver me from the hand of this Philistine'" (1 Sam. 17:34–37). Shepherds were known to be fearless defenders of their sheep.

A Psalm of David

It is surely not accidental that Psalm 23 is a psalm of David, the shepherd king. David knows what it is to be a shepherd. The psalm is his personal testimony to the Lord's unfailing faithfulness to him in all the highs and lows of his life as a believer. He also knew what it was to be a wandering sheep, to be an embattled sheep, and to be surrounded by enemies, even enemies within the Shepherd's sheepfold.

But to appreciate fully David's significance, we must understand that he is set before us in the pages of the Bible as a type of Christ. David is Israel's shepherd king, the servant king of Yahweh, the divine Shepherd of His people. In this office and role, David prefigured the Servant King of Yahweh, the Lord Jesus Christ. There is therefore a necessary twofold interpretation of the psalm that compels our attention. First, in Yahweh's care for David, His provision for all his needs, His guiding of him through life's darkest valley, His protection from surrounding enemies, and His bringing him ultimately into the joy and blessedness of His nearer presence, we see a prophetic outline of Yahweh's personal care and love for His Son—the perfect Shepherd King, the Lord Jesus Christ, the true Israel of God (Isa. 49:3). Second, the divine Shepherd who graciously and faithfully superintended King David's life is revealed in all His transcendent grace and sacrificial care in the life of God's incarnate Son, Jesus Christ. Jesus understood that He was "the good Shepherd" who had come to lay down His life for His sheep (see John 10:11–16).

A Psalm about Jesus Christ

It is impossible for a Christian to read this psalm and not imme-diately think of Jesus's self-description as the Good Shepherd who had come to lay down His life for His sheep (John 10:11).[2] Jesus is the Good Shepherd who personally knows His sheep

---

2. Jonathan Edwards has an excellent exposition of David as a type of Christ ("Types of the Messiah") in his volume on typology. There Edwards details the historico-typological parallels from which he sets out David, his life,

(John 10:3). He goes before them and, unlike the "hireling," He will not flee when He sees the marauding enemies of the sheep threaten to devour them (John 10:3, 12–13).

One of the Bible's inherent features is its slow, deliberate, increasingly enriching unfolding of the history of redemption. The first gospel promise of Genesis 3:15, "I will put enmity between you and the woman, and between your seed and her Seed; He shall bruise your head, and you shall bruise His heel," was both explicit and tantalizing. Who would this seed of the woman be? Throughout the Old Testament, the answer to that burning question is increasingly adumbrated. He would come from the tribe of Judah (Gen. 49:10–12). He would be a greater prophet than Moses (Deut. 18:15–19). He would be a priest, not from the tribe of Levi but after the order of Melchizedek (Ps. 110). He would be Immanuel, "God with us" (Isa. 7:14), and His name would be called "Wonderful, Counselor, Mighty God, Everlasting Father, Prince of Peace" (Isa. 9:6). He would be the perfectly faithful Shepherd Israel had never had (see Ezek. 34).

All these lines of trajectory find their convergence in the person of God's only begotten Son, the Lord Jesus Christ. He is the Lion of the tribe of Judah, God's final Word, the Prince of Peace, the Good Shepherd who had come to tend God's flock, see them brought safely into His sheepfold, and thereafter brought safely into God's nearer presence.

When Jesus said, "I am the good shepherd" (John 10:11), He knew what He was saying. He was identifying Himself as the long-promised Shepherd who would personally seek the

offices, and experiences as typological preparations for the Messiah. See volume 11 of *The Works of Edwards* (New Haven, Conn.: Yale University Press, 1993).

lost, bind up the broken, strengthen the sick, and destroy the fat and the strong.

Psalm 23 points beyond its immediate circumstance to the incarnate Lord of glory, who would do what no other shepherd could do: He would lay down His life as a sin-atoning sacrifice for His sheep, thereby securing their everlasting good.

A Psalm of Experiential Realism

Psalm 23 might appear to confront us with a problem. Are we to assume that what we read here was David's daily, unvarying experience? From David's life and from the many psalms he penned, we know he experienced more than "green pastures" and "still waters." Indeed, the opening words of the previous psalm, "My God, My God, why have You forsaken Me? Why are You so far from helping Me, and from the words of My groaning? O My God, I cry in the daytime, but You do not hear; and in the night season, and am not silent" (Ps. 22:1–2), eloquently speak of a time in David's life when green pastures and still waters were far from his experience. David's life as a man of faith was not even and untroubled.

We could say that Psalm 23 is but one snapshot of David's experience as a believer, and that would be true. But in penning this psalm, David not only speaks about the delights of green pastures and still waters but also writes about being led through the "valley of the shadow of death" (v. 4) and of being surrounded by "enemies" (v. 5).

Psalm 23 is neither idyllic nor unrealistic. David well understands that the life of faith is not an "even" life. The life of the perfect man of faith, the Good Shepherd Himself, Jesus

Christ, was not even and untroubled. He acknowledged that
His disciples had stayed with Him in His trials (Luke 22:28).
From the moment He entered into the public arena of His
ministry and mission, hostility and opposition were His daily
experience. The idea that the "normal Christian life" is a life
of unsullied joy and peace, if only we exercise enough faith, is
a blasphemy and a heresy.

No one has better understood this truth than the English
Puritan pastor John Owen. In his exposition of the believer's
sanctification, Owen writes, just as "the growth of plants is
not by a constant insensible progress…but…by sudden gusts
and motions," so "the growth of believers consists principally
in some intense vigorous actings of grace on great occasions."[3]

It has pleased the Lord not to give us steady, uninterrupted
growth in grace; rather, He is pleased to have us cry to Him,
wait on Him, and seek His face, often in the midst of trials,
before He grants us to grow in likeness to the Savior—if
nothing else, to humble us and keep us dependent on Him.

As an insightful pastor, Owen proceeds to answer a pressing pastoral question: "I do not see much, if any, growth in
grace in my life: am I therefore devoid of the root of holiness?" Owen's response is measured, searching, and pastorally
reassuring. He says, first of all, "every one in whom is a prin-
ciple of spiritual life, who is born of God, in whom the work
of sanctification is begun, if it be not gradually carried on
in him, if he thrive not in grace and holiness, if he go not
from strength to strength, it is ordinarily from his own sinful

3. John Owen, *Pneumatologia, or, A Discourse concerning the Holy Spirit*
(London: Banner of Truth, 1965), 3:397.

negligence."[4] Owen urges us, then, to search our hearts if we appear to be regressing in holiness and to cast off the sin that so easily besets us. Second, Owen proceeds quickly to balance what he has just said: it is one thing for holiness to be present and another for the believer to be conscious of it. Indeed, continues Owen, "there may be seasons wherein sincere, humble believers may be obliged to believe the increase and growth of (holiness) in them when they perceive it not, so as to be sensible of it."[5] Owen never forgets he is a pastor, writing for Christ's lambs. He is quick to reassure struggling saints: "What shall we say, then? is there no sincere holiness where…decays are found? God forbid."[6] Progress is erratic and "horticultural," not even and "mechanical."

This truth could be used by the sinfully negligent to placate their conscience: "The way of holiness is erratic and uneven. I must expect to regress and even grow cold in my affections; things will change for the better, sometime." Such thinking reflects either a deeply backslidden condition or, more seriously, a yet unregenerate life. A true Christian will always grieve over his or her lack of progress in the grace and knowledge of the Savior, never simply shrug their shoulders with the thought, "Que sera, sera" ("What will be, will be").

Living and Dying
Throughout the Bible we discover that the life of faith in God experiences two synchronous realities: the believer is always being led in Christ's triumphal procession (2 Cor. 2:14) and,

---

4. Owen, *Pneumatologia*, in *Works*, 3:400.
5. Owen, *Pneumatologia*, in *Works*, 3:401.
6. Owen, *Pneumatologia*, in *Works*, 3:404.

at the same time, afflicted, perplexed, persecuted, struck down, "always carrying about in the body the dying of the Lord Jesus" (2 Cor. 4:8–12). This "double grace" should not surprise us; it was the shape of the earthly life of the Lord Jesus Christ. This is the shape of the Christian's union with Christ. It is this shape, first etched in the holy humanity of Christ, that the Holy Spirit comes to replicate in the lives of everyone whom He has united by faith to the Savior.

John Calvin used two vivid Latin words to express this synchronous reality lived out in the people of God: *mortificatio* and *vivificatio* (mortification and vivification). Calvin understands that sanctification, growth in grace, has two parts, both of which happen to us by our union with Christ.[7] These occur synchronously and continuously throughout the Christian life. In *mortificatio*, we seek, by the help of the Holy Spirit, to put remaining sin to death (Rom. 8:13). In *vivificatio*, we seek, again by the help of the Holy Spirit, to experience and express in our lives the risen, triumphant life of our Savior. This is the principal shape of the believing life.

A Psalm of Personal "Exodus"

In Genesis 3 we read of Adam and Eve being exiled from the garden of Eden. Because they willfully disobeyed, God cast them out and set cherubim over the entrance to guard the way back to the Tree of Life. If humanity was ever to be restored to God, there would need to be "an exodus back to

---

7. John Calvin, *Institutes of the Christian Religion* (Philadelphia: Westminster Press, 1960), 3.3.2, 9.

God, a deliverance out of exile."[8] In the book of Exodus, we read of a second exile—Israel's exodus, its deliverance by the hand of God from its slavery in Egypt. This moment of divine, sovereign power and mercy pervades the whole of the Old Testament and is highlighted in the New Testament by Paul in 1 Corinthians 5:7: "Christ, our Passover, was sacrificed for us." But even more momentous was the exodus accomplished by the Lord Jesus Christ. In the Savior's epochal meeting with Moses and Elijah on the Mount of Transfiguration, Luke tells us that they "spoke of His decease which He was about to accomplish at Jerusalem" (Luke 9:31). The word *decease* literally means "exodus" (ἔξοδον, exhodon). In Jesus, God would effect an infinitely greater deliverance than He had under Moses.

The truths embedded in these great moments of exodus in redemptive history are reflected in every life that God makes His own. Every saved sinner has been "exodused," rescued, from sin and death and hell and has been brought into the freedom of the children of God (Rom. 8:21). In Psalm 23, David is writing as a rescued sinner who has been brought by the heavenly Shepherd into the security and freedom of His sheepfold.

If you have not been "exodused" from the guilt, tyranny, and condemnation of sin and have not been brought by God's glorious grace in Christ into the security and blessedness of His family, your great need is to have your sad and tragic condition remedied. There is but one remedy, the Passover Lamb who was sacrificed to take away the sin of the world. He,

---

8. L. Michael Morales, *Exodus Old and New: A Biblical Theology of Redemption* (Downers Grove, Ill.: InterVarsity Press, 2020), 8.

God's own Son, Jesus Christ, says to you, "Come to Me, all you who labor and are heavy laden, and I will give you rest. Take My yoke upon you and learn from Me, for I am gentle and lowly in heart, and you will find rest for your souls. For My yoke is easy and My burden is light" (Matt. 11:28–30).

John Owen wrote, "Unacquaintedness with our mercies, our privileges, is our sin as well as our trouble. We hearken not to the voice of the Spirit which is given unto us, 'that we may know the things that are freely bestowed on us of God.'"[9] My hope is that as we reflect on the psalm verse by verse, we will become better acquainted with our God-given mercies and see how rich and vastly blessed and privileged the believer's life is while also learning that the life of faith is lived out in the midst of dark valleys, surrounded by God's enemies. Above all, however, my hope is that we will see how personally committed the Lord is to care for, protect, and bring His people to be with Him in the glory of His heaven.

---

9. Owen, *Communion with God*, in *Works*, 2:32.

Questions

1. Why did God include the book of Psalms in the Bible?

2. In what ways does Psalm 23 point us forward to the Lord Jesus Christ?

3. What is meant by *experiential religion*?

4. How would you define and describe what the Bible means by *sanctification*?

5. What does it mean in practice for the Lord to be your shepherd?

The Lord
Loves His Sheep

The LORD is my shepherd; I shall not want.

David's Faith

The opening words of the psalm are eloquent in their simplicity and wonder. David is celebrating his greatest privilege: "The Lord is my shepherd." Throughout the psalm, God's "personal name," Yahweh, is used. This is the name that speaks of God's covenant love for and commitment to His people (see Ex. 3:14). David is making the staggering assertion that the Lord, the sovereign Creator of the heavens and the earth, the God who is from everlasting to everlasting, the high and holy One who inhabits eternity, is "my shepherd."

David does not tell us when the Lord became his Shepherd. In the previous psalm David wrote, "You are He who took Me out of the womb; You made Me trust while on My mother's breasts. I was cast upon You from birth. From My mother's womb You have been My God" (Ps. 22:9–10). Throughout the Bible, there is little interest in when and how anyone is converted. The Holy Spirit's work of regeneration is hidden from view (John 3:7–8). What is of the greatest concern is that someone truly is a believer and that their life shows that they are. The great sin of God's old covenant people was covenantal presumption. They prized their covenant privileges but not the gracious God who blessed them with those privileges. Gospel privileges of themselves do not make us right with God. John the Baptist confronted the spiritual leaders of God's church with their unregenerate lives: "Brood of vipers! Who warned you to flee from the wrath to come? Therefore bear fruits worthy of repentance, and do not think to say to yourselves, 'We have Abraham as our father.' For I say to you that God is able to raise up children to Abraham from these stones. And even now the ax is laid to the root of the trees. Therefore every tree which does not bear good fruit is cut down and thrown into the fire" (Matt. 3:7–10). These men had all the covenant privileges that God had graciously given to His people (see Rom. 9:4–5), but their hearts were unrenewed; they gave no evidence of saving repentance.

David is not comforting himself by looking back to a moment when he "gave his heart to the Lord." He says, "The Lord *is* my shepherd." A Christian's testimony to the Lord and His saving grace will never dwell in the past, however dramatic the past may have been. The vital thing is that *today* your hope and trust rest alone in the Lord and in His grace to you in His Son, Jesus Christ.

A Vivid Picture

In speaking of the Lord as his Shepherd, David is using the most intimate and evocative of metaphors. A sheep without a shepherd is a pitiful sight. It is an open prey to wild animals. It has little sense of lurking danger. Later the prophet Isaiah likened himself and all people to sheep who had gone astray and were mired in inextricable lostness (Isa. 53:6). It was the sad and sorry condition of the crowds who followed Him that deeply moved the heart of the Savior. Matthew records that "when He saw the multitudes, He was moved with compassion for them, because they were weary and scattered, like sheep having no shepherd" (Matt. 9:36).

David, with all his kingly and covenantal privileges, understands he is like a sheep. He knows he is vulnerable, incapable of knowing what is best and right. He knows that left to himself life would at best be intolerable and at worst impossible. But David had learned as a young man that he had a great unseen helper (read 1 Sam. 17:45–46).

Unbounded Assurance

The hugely important thing to notice here is David's unambiguous confidence: "The Lord *is* my shepherd." There is nothing tentative here, no ifs, buts, or maybes. David speaks simply, boldly, and unambiguously, with a self-conscious confidence.

At the Reformation, the Roman Church considered the Protestants' teaching on assurance of salvation to be one of its greatest heresies. If men and women could be assured before God of their salvation, where would that leave the church and its multitude of sacraments and penances? The priest would no longer be a conveyor of forgiveness, he would be "simply" a declarer of God's truth! Assurance that almighty God is yours and that you are His, that you truly do belong to His sheepfold, is not a privilege for a spiritual elite. No. It is the birthright of everyone born of the Spirit. Jesus did not teach His disciples to pray, "Our Father, if you really are our Father." He taught His disciples to pray with childlike confidence that the great God of heaven truly was their Father because they belonged to His Son.

However, this does not mean that all Christians possess unclouded assurance. Assurance may be the birthright of every forgiven sinner, but forgiven sinners still sin. Sin yet remains to trouble, discourage, and even dishearten the best of Christians. The Westminster Confession of Faith memorably enshrined this truth in chapter 18, "Of the Assurance of Grace and Salvation":

> True believers may have the assurance of their salvation divers ways shaken, diminished, and intermitted; as, by negligence in preserving of it, by falling into some special sin, which woundeth the conscience and grieveth the Spirit; by some sudden or vehement temptation, by God's withdrawing the light of His countenance, and suffering even such as fear Him to walk in darkness and to have no light: yet are they never utterly destitute of that seed of God, and life of faith, that love of Christ and the brethren, that sincerity of heart, and conscience of duty, out of which, by the operation of the Spirit, this assurance may, in due time, be revived; and by the which, in the mean time, they are supported from utter despair. (WCF 18.4)

But it must never be forgotten that assurance is not a privilege enjoyed only by elite Christians. No good father wants his children to doubt he is their father and that they are his dearly loved children. Even when he chastens them, he does so as a father who loves them and who always has their best at heart (see Heb. 12:5–11). David knew the heavenly Shepherd's sore chastising (see Ps. 51), but he never doubted that he was, by God's grace, one of the heavenly Shepherd's sheep.

The Good Shepherd

The conviction that God is the divine Shepherd of believers is a theme that runs through the whole of Scripture. Ezekiel 34 is perhaps the high point of this teaching in the Old Testament, but the Shepherd-sheep relationship reaches its climax in Jesus's teaching in John 10:11–16:

> I am the good shepherd. The good shepherd gives His life for the sheep. But a hireling, he who is not the shepherd, one who does not own the sheep, sees the wolf coming and leaves the sheep and flees; and the wolf catches the sheep and scatters them. The hireling flees because he is a hireling and does not care about the sheep. I am the good shepherd; and I know My sheep, and am known by My own. As the Father knows Me, even so I know the Father; and I lay down My life for the sheep. And other sheep I have which are not of this fold; them also I must bring, and they will hear My voice; and there will be one flock and one shepherd.

Because the living God is their Shepherd, believers can be assured they have a Shepherd who will stop at nothing, who will do anything, to secure the good of His sheep (John 10:11).

But the Bible is no less insistent in telling us that our sin has separated us from God and brought us under His condemnation: "The soul that sins shall die"; "The wages of sin is death"; by nature we are "children of wrath like the rest of mankind." If "all we like sheep have gone astray" (Isa. 53:6), what hope then is there for any of us?

Yet there is hope for all of us. Jesus Himself explains how it is that we can have hope: "I am the good shepherd. The good shepherd gives His life for the sheep" (John 10:11). The cross is where we see the Shepherd's great, restoring, rescuing love for His sheep. There God the Father "laid on Him the iniquity of us all" (Isa. 53:6). This is why the heavenly Father loves His Son (John 10:17). He loved Him from all eternity as God the Son, who ever was in the bosom of His Father (John 1:1, 18). But now as the Good Shepherd who would lay down His life as a sin-atoning sacrifice for His sheep, the people given to Him by His Father (John 17:2), the Father pours down His love on His obedient-unto-death Son.

A Comforting Deduction

From his assurance that the Lord is his Shepherd, David makes a comforting deduction: "I shall not want"; that is, "I shall lack nothing." David is confident that because he is one of the heavenly Shepherd's sheep, he will lack no good thing. If the Lord God Almighty is his shepherd; his loving, caring helper and provider; the God of covenant faithfulness, then David is assured he will lack nothing. He is drawing a believing deduction from the wonderful truth that the Lord is his Shepherd. If he truly is one of the heavenly Shepherd's own sheep, loved and cared for, is it possible that He will withhold any good thing from David?

David's believing deduction flows out of his doctrine of God. I have often thought of the words in Psalm 119:68, "You are good, and do good." It is because the Lord is good that He does good. He cannot not do good. Goodness natively belongs to who He is. All His ways are good because He is good. It is our doctrine of God that alone will sustain us in the midst of life's often bewildering providences. Doctrine matters. One of the most significant moments in a young believer's life is when it dawns on him or her that doctrine is instinct with life.

Theology is not a mere collection of facts about God. Martin Bucer, the Strasburg Reformer who greatly influenced John Calvin, understood the practical nature of biblical truth: "True theology is not theoretical, but practical. The end of it is living, that is to live a godly life."[1] Calvin himself no less grasped that doctrine was instinct with life: "For true doctrine," he wrote, "is not a matter of the tongue, but of life; neither is Christian doctrine grasped only by the intellect and memory, as truth is grasped in other fields of study. Rather, doctrine is rightly received when it takes possession of the entire soul and finds a dwelling place and shelter in the most intimate affections of the heart."[2]

Paul makes an identical practical observation in Romans 8:31–32. He is arguing from the greater to the lesser: if, because of His great love for us, God did not spare/withhold His own Son from the sin-bearing death of the cross, is it conceivable that He would then withhold anything good from us? On the contrary, He will "freely [graciously] give us all things." Obviously not all things that we desire, for the good reason that not one of us knows what is truly best for us; we are creatures of the moment, incapable of knowing what is for our present good, never mind our eternal good. How many daily bless the Lord that He did not give them things that at one time they passionately pleaded for? Rather,

---

1. Quoted in Brian Lugioyo, *Martin Bucer's Doctrine of Justification: Reformation Theology and Early Modern Irenicism*, Oxford Studies in Historical Theology (Oxford: Oxford University Press, 2010), 54.

2. Calvin, *Institutes of the Christian Religion*, 3.6.4.

the "all things" that the Lord will give us are those things that will sanctify us, fit us for glory, and make us useful servants of His grace here and now.

Many Christians cry out for practical help in living the life of faith in Jesus Christ. The greatest help they can be given is to set before them the expansive, soul-nourishing, mind-and-heart-elevating truth about God and His covenant-pledged love to His children. This is why the preaching of the cross must ever lie at the heart of any authentic gospel ministry. When Paul wrote, "we preach Christ crucified," the defining note of his preaching and of the gospel of the God of grace, he was telling us that this multifaceted doctrine is both the central message of Christianity and its life-giving, life-changing dynamic.

It is one of Satan's tactics to suggest that God is not wholly good, that He is less than He says He is, that He does withhold what is good from us. This is how he seduced Adam and Eve in the garden of Eden. What are you to do when he subtly suggests to you that God is less than His Word says He is? We hurl at him the message—the doctrine of the cross of our Lord Jesus Christ. The doctrine of Christ crucified is the bulwark of our souls.

John Owen well understood the practical importance of the believer grasping this truth:

> How few of the saints are experimentally acquainted with this privilege of holding immediate communion with the Father in love! With what anxious doubt-ful thoughts do they look upon him! What fears, what questionings are there, of his good-will and kindness! At the best, many think there is no sweetness at all in

> God towards us, but what is purchased at the high price of the blood of Jesus. It is true, that alone is the way of communication; but the free fountain and spring of all is in the bosom of the Father.[3]

It is one thing to be notionally, theologically convinced of this and another to be personally, experientially acquainted with this truth. The gospel of God (Rom. 1:1) is the power of God for salvation (Rom. 1:16). It is not a set of theorems we are to acknowledge; it is a dynamic that we are to experience.

So, is the Lord your Shepherd? Has He become your shepherd? Does your life give evidence that He is your Shepherd? Have you come to see yourself, as the Bible pictures all of us, as a lost sheep, in desperate need of a merciful, kind, and caring shepherd? (Read Matt. 9:36; Luke 15:3–7.) We live in a world full of lost sheep, wandering aimlessly, heading for the precipice of everlasting destruction. Your and my greatest need in life is a gracious, loving, kind heavenly Shepherd. Jesus said, "I am the good shepherd. The good shepherd gives His life for the sheep" (John 10:11). To God be all praise and glory.

---

3. Owen, *Communion with God*, in *Works*, 2:32.

Questions

1. Why does the Bible describe unbelievers and believers as sheep?

2. Does assurance of salvation belong to the essence of saving faith? Explain your answer.

3. In what ways does the Lord shepherd His sheep?

4. How do we become one of the Lord's sheep?

The Heavenly Shepherd Provides for His Sheep

He makes me to lie down in green pastures;
He leads me beside the still waters.

The opening words of Psalm 23 are among the most memorable in the Bible. They are richly reassuring, wonderfully comforting, and theologically elevating. Throughout the psalm David is celebrating the lovingkindness of his God. There are no petitions, no intercessions, no complaints. David simply celebrates the Lord and His unfailing goodness and mercy (see v. 6).

From verse 2, David begins to unpack what it means for him not to be in want, to lack nothing. He has told us that the Lord is his Shepherd, that he has a personal, divine helper and provider. But what does that mean for him? How does that truth impact and shape his life?

Before we continue I want to say again that this is but one psalm out of one hundred and fifty psalms. In some of his psalms, David writes very differently. In Psalm 22:1 he cries out that God has forsaken him. In Psalm 28:1–3, he pleads with the Lord not to be deaf to his cries and not to drag him off "with the wicked and with the workers of iniquity."

In Psalm 10:1 he asks, "Why do You stand afar off, O LORD? Why do You hide in times of trouble?"

The Psalms remind us that the life of faith is not always marked by tranquility and lavish, tenderly provided provision. The life of the prototypical man of faith, Jesus Christ, was marked by disappointment, difficulty, hostility, threats, and unrelenting opposition from the devil. You must guard against having unreal (that is, unbiblical) expectations for your life.

How, then, are we to understand what David writes here? How are we to translate David's pastoral imagery into our daily experience? There are perhaps two dominant thoughts being highlighted: the provision the Lord supplies and the rest He gives.

The Heavenly Shepherd's Provision

Because He is the ultimate Good Shepherd, the Lord richly provides for the needs of His sheep. The imagery of green pastures and quiet waters, or waters of rest, is intended to highlight God's abundant care for His sheep. He is a shepherd who personally leads His sheep to the nourishing and refreshing provision that will strengthen and sustain them.

The climate in the Near East can be brutal, and the summers can be especially arid. As a student, I spent two months in Tiberias in northern Israel and woke up every morning to unrelenting heat. (I had no air-conditioning! If my reading and preparations were not completed by 10 a.m., this Scotsman, used to 60°F in the summer, not 100°F, would wilt in the heat.) Green pastures and flowing streams of water would be what every good shepherd sought for his sheep. As he led his sheep, he would know where best to provide for their needs.

What we now need to ask is this: What does this heavenly Shepherd provide for His sheep? How are we to translate the pastoral imagery of green pastures and quiet waters into the truths they are pictorially conveying? Clearly David is thinking about how the Lord richly provides for his daily needs as one of His sheep. How, then, does the Lord provide for the spiritual nourishment of His people?

His Written Word

The heavenly Shepherd provides for His sheep by the means of His written Word. Jesus's response to the devil when He was tempted by him in the wilderness at the outset of His public ministry is significant. When the Evil One tempted the Savior to turn stones into bread to satisfy His hunger, He replied, "It is written, 'Man shall not live by bread alone, but by every word that proceeds from the mouth of God'" (Matt. 4:4). God's written Word, infallibly inspired by the Holy Spirit (2 Tim. 3:16; 2 Peter 1:19–21), is the revelation of His saving wisdom, love, grace, and goodness. In His Word, God says to us, "Behold your God. See how great and gracious I am. See how majestic and powerful I am. See how pledged I am to secure your good in the incarnation, life, death, and resurrection of My Son, to bless you with every spiritual blessing. Having not spared My own Son, but delivered Him up for the salvation of My sheep, do you think I would withhold any good thing from you?" (see Rom. 8:32).

In Psalm 19:10, the sweet, nourishing grace of God's teaching, His Torah, is beautifully depicted: "More to be desired are they than gold, yea, than much fine gold; sweeter also than honey and the honeycomb." The psalmist is telling us two significant things about God's law, His instruction: its inestimable worth and its inestimable value.

Its Inestimable Worth

It is "more to be desired" than gold. The meaning of the Hebrew could perhaps be better expressed, "more to be desired than gold, yes, and deservedly so." What is the psalmist speaking about? The entirety of God's revealed truth as he knew it. He did not possess what we possess, the written Word of God in its fullest revelation. He is celebrating the Torah, most probably the five books of Moses. The question we need to ask is, Why? Why is it more to be desired than gold, than much fine gold? Essentially because of what it is, the Word of God. Into a world shrouded with lies, half-truths, and self-interest, God has spoken. Because we have short memories, long tongues, and deceitful hearts, God has equipped and inspired men to write down His revelation (2 Peter 1:20–21). Because it is preeminently the Word of God, His personally breathed-out word, it can be trusted absolutely. In Psalm 119:72, the psalmist tells us that the Torah is "the law of Your mouth." It is this truth that Jesus affirms in Matthew 4:4: "Man shall not live by bread alone, but by every word that proceeds from the mouth of God."

Its Inestimable Value

The inestimable value of the word that has proceeded from God's mouth lies specifically in what it actually teaches. Out of His own mouth, God tells us about Himself and His saving, cosmic purposes. In Genesis 1, He tells us He is the sovereign Creator and Lord of all things seen and unseen. In Exodus 3, He tells us He is the self-existent God who has neither beginning of days nor end of life. In Isaiah 6, He tells us He is the thrice Holy One before whom the unfallen heavenly beings bow down and ceaselessly worship. In Genesis 3, He tells us of His promise to send a Rescuer from the seed of woman who would defeat the devil. In the sacrificial system that He bequeathed to His covenant people (read Exodus and Leviticus), He set forth the way of salvation through sacrificial, substitutionary blood atonement. Later, especially in Isaiah, He tells us that the promised Rescuer would be born of a virgin and be given the name Immanuel, "God with us" (7:14). Perhaps most remarkably, in Isaiah's Servant Songs, He draws us four word pictures of this Immanuel on whom the Lord would lay "the iniquity of us all" (53:6). Finally, in Isaiah 66, He tells us about His ultimate purpose to make a "new heavens" and a "new earth" (v. 22; 2 Peter 3; Rev. 22).

Word and Spirit

This leaves us asking, with John Calvin, the question, "How can this be known?"[1] The answer Calvin gives is the one Scripture itself gives: "by the revelation of the...Spirit."[2] The Word of God without the Spirit of God is a dead letter. It is more than possible for the preaching of the gospel to come to men and women "in word only" (1 Thess. 1:5). John Calvin famously likened the Word of God to spectacles that enable us to see the truth. But Calvin understood that without the ministry of the Holy Spirit opening our sin-blinded eyes to

---

1. John Calvin, *Commentaries* (Grand Rapids: Baker, 1993), 21:249.
2. Calvin, *Commentaries*, 21:249.

see, God's Word would remain a dead letter to us. This is why he wrote of the *Internum testimonium Spiritus Sancti*—the internal testimony, or witness, of the Holy Spirit. We need the Spirit to invade our lives and plant within us a new heart, uniting us to Jesus Christ in the new birth, enlightening our understanding, enabling us not only to hear the gospel but to believe the Savior held out to us in the gospel. This is precisely what Paul is saying in 1 Corinthians 2:11–12: "No one knows the things of God except the Spirit of God. Now we have received, not the spirit of the world, but the Spirit who is from God, that we might know the things that have been freely given to us by God." This is why the psalmist prayed, "Open my eyes, that I may see wondrous things from Your law" (Ps. 119:18). The psalmist was a believer, a truly regenerate man, but he acknowledged his absolute dependence on the Holy Spirit to give him spiritual understanding.

When Jesus encountered Nicodemus (John 3), he instinctively knew that the problem with this man, "the teacher of Israel" (v. 10), was not that he lacked intelligence but that he lacked the Holy Spirit: "Most assuredly, I say to you, unless one is born of water and the Spirit, he cannot enter the kingdom of God. That which is born of the flesh is flesh, and that which is born of the Spirit is spirit. Do not marvel that I said to you, 'You must be born again.' The wind blows where it wishes, and you hear the sound of it, but cannot tell where it comes from and where it goes. So is everyone who is born of the Spirit" (vv. 5–8). Christianity is natively "Pneumatic." The Reformed faith, Calvinism if you like, is profoundly shaped by the person, ministry, and indwelling presence of God the Holy Spirit. He has come, however, not to glorify Himself but to bring glory to His "best friend" (a *parakletos* in the ancient world was often a man's best friend), the Lord Jesus Christ: "He will glorify Me, for He will take of what is Mine and declare it to you" (John 16:14).

In his magisterial work on the Holy Spirit, John Owen wrote these striking words: "He that would utterly separate the Spirit from the word had as good burn his Bible. The bare letter of the New Testament will no more ingenerate faith and obedience in the souls of men…than the letter of the Old Testament."[3] Owen is reminding us, albeit in the most dramatic way, that the Word of God is never to be separated from the Spirit of God.

In his comments on "All Scripture is given by inspiration of God" (2 Tim. 3:16), Calvin writes, "The same Spirit, therefore, who made Moses and the prophets certain of their calling, now also testifies to our hearts…. Accordingly, we need not wonder if there are many who doubt as to the Author of the Scripture; for, although the majesty of God is displayed in it, yet none but those who have been enlightened by the Holy Spirit have eyes to perceive what ought, indeed, to have been visible to all, and yet is visible to the elect alone."[4]

One of the marks of a person's election by God to salvation is that they gladly affirm with their minds and hearts the full authority and truthfulness of God's written word. They affirm with their Savior that "man shall not live by bread alone, but by every word that proceeds from the mouth of God" (Matt. 4:4).

---

3. Owen, *Pneumatologia*, in *Works*, 3:192.
4. Calvin, *Commentaries*, 21:249.

Its Experienced Delight

The inestimable value of God's Word is matched by the personal delight believers have in its intrinsic truth. God's truth is "sweeter than honey." God's law, His teaching, is not a bare list of theological truths. It is not a compendium of theological theorems we have to understand and give assent to. Yes, God's truth is propositional. His revealed truth has a defined form or shape (Rom. 6:17). It is a nonnegotiable body of divinity (Jude 3). But it is truth that is nourishing, refreshing, and sweet to the taste (Ps. 34:8). It is sweet to read about the "I am." It is sweet to read that although my "sins are like scarlet, they shall be as white as snow; though they are red like crimson, they shall be as wool" (Isa. 1:18). It is sweet to read God's "exceedingly great and precious promises" (2 Peter 1:4) that belong to believers. It is sweet to read of the "inheritance incorruptible and undefiled and that does not fade away, reserved in heaven for you, who are kept by the power of God through faith for salvation ready to be revealed in the last time" (1 Peter 1:4–5). The word of God is true and authoritative, and it is no less sweet and full of relish (a word John Owen often used).

Thomas Boston was, by common consent, one of the greatest ministers raised up by God in his church in Scotland. Around the year 1700, Boston, who was a faithful minister of the Word, came across a book that transformed his ministry: *The Marrow of Modern Divinity*.[5] After reading *The Marrow*, Boston wrote, "It speedily gave a tincture to my preaching."[6]

---

5. You can read Boston's own account of how *The Marrow* impacted his preaching and pastoral ministry in his *Memoirs* (Edinburgh: Banner of Truth, 1988), xxvii, 169.

6. Boston, *Memoirs*, 169.

In a remarkable way, the Holy Spirit gave to Boston a new, fresh relish in reading and preaching God's Word—a "tincture" his congregation immediately recognized. Let me address a question to my fellow ministers of the Word: Do your congregations discern such a tincture or relish in your preaching ministry?

Scripture and Confessions of Faith

The book you are even now consulting as you read these words has come from the mouth of the Lord. This is why John Calvin could write, "We owe to the Scripture the same reverence as we owe to God; because it has proceeded from him alone, and has nothing belonging to man mixed with it."[7] This makes the Bible trustworthy and absolutely authoritative. The Westminster divines wisely stated in the Westminster Shorter Catechism,

> Q. 2. What rule has God given to direct us how we may glorify and enjoy Him?
>
> A. The word of God, which is contained in the Scriptures of the Old and New Testaments, is the only rule to direct us how we may glorify and enjoy Him.

Notice, "the only rule." However excellent and helpful confessions of faith and catechisms are for instructing Christians, it must never be forgotten that they are helps and that God's written Word alone is our rule of faith and life. In chapter 31 of the Westminster Confession of Faith, "Of Synods and Councils," the divines wrote, "All synods or councils, since the

---

7. Calvin, *Commentaries*, 21:249.

Apostles' times, whether general or particular, may err; and many have erred. Therefore they are not to be made the rule of faith, or practice; but to be used as a help in both" (WCF 31.3). The divines understood that unlike God's written word, their confession was not infallible.

This conviction marked the magisterial Reformers and the confessions of faith they produced. The Scots Confession (1560), most probably shaped by John Knox, includes this famous statement: "Protesting, that if any man will note in this our Confession any article or sentence repugning [contrary] to God's holy word, that it would please him of his gentleness, and for Christian charity's sake, to admonish us of the same in writ; and We of our honour and fidelity do promise unto him satisfaction from the mouth of God (that is, from his holy Scriptures), or else reformation of that which he shall prove to be amiss" (preface to the Scots Confession).

How the Lord Leads His Sheep
The heavenly Shepherd leads and never drives His sheep. In the Middle East, the shepherd leads and his sheep follow. This is a truth Jesus highlights in John 10:4–5: "And when he [the Shepherd] brings out his own sheep, he goes before them; and the sheep follow him, for they know his voice. Yet they will by no means follow a stranger, but will flee from him, for they do not know the voice of strangers." One of the telling ways to distinguish between the activity of Satan and the work of God is embedded in Jesus's statement. Good and godly shepherds, Jesus preeminently, lead their sheep; they go before them, never drive them.

It is striking and significant that in the first of Isaiah's Servant Songs, we are told that the Lord's Servant is His answer to the idol worship and idolaters that so defile the world (The "Behold" that begins chapter 42, is the third in a triad of "Beholds": "Behold ye are of nothing…Behold they are all vanity…Behold my servant" (Isa. 41:24, 29; 42:1 KJV). What we are to behold in the Lord's Servant, among other significant things, is that "He will not cry out, nor raise His voice, nor cause His voice to be heard in the street. A bruised reed He will not break, and smoking flax He will not quench" (Isa. 42:2–3). A line from the hymn "I Greet Thee Who My Sure Redeemer Art" (often attributed to John Calvin) captures the thought beautifully: "No harshness hast thou and no bitterness." This servant, God's Messiah, His chosen One in whom His soul delights, the Good Shepherd Himself, never deals harshly with any of His sheep. He never drives; He always gently leads.

But the Good Shepherd's gentleness should never be confused with weakness. His care for His sheep is so genuine that, when necessary, He will chastise them. The writer to the Hebrews impresses this truth on us: "My son, do not despise the chastening of the LORD, nor be discouraged when you are rebuked by Him; for whom the LORD loves He chastens, and scourges every son whom He receives" (Heb. 12:5–6, quoting Prov. 3:11–12; Job 5:17; Ps. 94:12). This is how the perfect Good Shepherd leads His flock; this is how all undershepherds are to lead the precious sheep entrusted to their care.

But, more practically, *how* does the Lord "lead" His sheep?

Personal Leading

The Good Shepherd leads His flock *personally*. Our heavenly Shepherd does not delegate this work of shepherding to any man or angel. Understand what I am saying. Of course the Lord raises up men and uses them as undershepherds in caring for His flock. Peter writes to the church's elders in the dispersion, "Shepherd the flock of God which is among you, serving as overseers, not by compulsion but willingly, not for dishonest gain but eagerly; nor as being lords over those entrusted to you, but being examples to the flock; and when the Chief Shepherd appears, you will receive the crown of glory that does not fade away" (1 Peter 5:2–4). But then he proceeds to speak of Jesus as the church's "Chief Shepherd" (v. 4). In his commentary on this verse, John Calvin wrote, "It ought to be also observed that he calls Christ the chief Pastor; for we are to rule the Church under him and in his name, in no other way but that he should be still really the Pastor."[8]

This commitment of God to shepherd His flock personally is the great refrain throughout Ezekiel 34. In verses 11–17, the Lord tells His people seventeen times that He personally ("I Myself," v. 11) will shepherd His chosen flock.

There is nothing remote or clinical or cavalier about how the heavenly Shepherd leads His sheep. Each one is precious in His sight. We are the apple of His eye (Ps. 17:8). Even more remarkably, we read in Zephaniah that the Lord personally rejoices over His people with "gladness" and with "singing" and that He calms our troubled souls with "His love"

---

8. Calvin, *Commentaries*, 22:146.

(Zeph. 3:17). This Shepherd makes the care of His sheep His personal pleasure.

Individual Leading

The Good Shepherd leads His flock *individually*. The Lord leads His people corporately. He has one flock, one family. But each individual within that community of faith is personally led by the Good Shepherd. Jesus's words in John 10:14, "I know my sheep," do not refer to a bare, clinical knowledge of who they are. His knowledge of His sheep is intimate: He formed you personally in your mother's womb; He ordained all your days before you were born; He knows the number of hairs on your head; He knows your every need. Isn't it amazing the way shepherds seem to know their sheep by name? Your gracious Shepherd knows every detail of your life. He knows your weaknesses, your failures, your temptations, your hopes, your disappointments, your passions and longings, the struggles you face, the joys you experience! You are not a faceless number among God's elect.

In His every dealing with His sheep, the heavenly Shepherd devotes Himself to each one individually. There is nothing monochrome or formulaic about the Lord's care for His own precious sheep. He does not have a preset mold that He squeezes every one of His dearly loved sheep into. Every believer is unique, and the Lord tailors His leading to that divinely ordained uniqueness.

Tender and Gentle Leading

The Good Shepherd leads His flock tenderly and gently. In Isaiah 40:11, we are given a beautiful description of the almighty, sovereign Lord's gentleness with His sheep: "He will feed His flock like a shepherd; He will gather the lambs with His arm, and carry them in His bosom, and gently lead those who are with young." These words ought to be engraved on the minds and hearts of every man set apart to shepherd God's sheep. No matter how bold and outgoing his temperament, every undershepherd is to model in his life and echo in his ministrations the "grace of the Lord Jesus Christ." Tenderness and gentleness are not primarily personality traits; they are spiritual graces. What the Holy Spirit first etched in the holy humanity of the Savior, He comes to replicate (to use John Calvin's word) in the lives of everyone united to Him, not least in the lives of those men who have been called and set apart to represent Him among His people.

Jesus could be fierce with the enemies of the gospel, especially when those enemies were found within the visible covenant fellowship of His church. But to His blood-redeemed people, He was always gentle, unthreatening, patient. That did not mean He could not, and would not when necessary, be strong. On one memorable occasion He said to Peter, "Get behind Me, Satan! You are an offense to Me, for you are not mindful of the things of God, but the things of men" (Matt. 16:23). Actually, Jesus could have said something more awful: "Get behind me, Peter!"

Persevering Leading

The Good Shepherd leads His flock perseveringly. In His parable of the lost sheep in Luke 15, Jesus tells us that the man who had lost his sheep would "go after the one which is lost until he finds it" (Luke 15:4). Jesus will not lose one of the sheep given to Him by His Father.

There is an old gospel hymn, "The Ninety and Nine," that was sung at many of Billy Graham's gospel rallies. The hymn begins with the words "There were ninety and nine that safely lay in the shelter of the fold."[9] It is a very evocative picture but sadly not one that is true to the parable Jesus taught. In the parable, Jesus tells us that the shepherd left the ninety-nine, not in the shelter of the fold but "in the wilderness," to go after the one sheep that was lost (Luke 15:4). What right-thinking shepherd would leave his flock in the open country, vulnerable to attacks, just to find one that was lost? This heavenly Shepherd.

This is the persevering commitment that our heavenly Shepherd pledges to His sheep. No matter what it will take, He will search and search until He finds every one of His lost sheep. This should be the most wonderful of encouragements for every Christian. Not one of the Shepherd's sheep will be lost. On the day when our Savior descends from the heavens with a shout, not one of those He ransomed with His precious blood will be missing. The doctrine of the perseverance of the saints should always be presented with its double dynamic: we are called to persevere faithfully to the end, and the Lord will enable us by His grace so to persevere. Paul beautifully captures this double dynamic in Philippians 2:12–13: "Work out your own salvation with fear and trembling; for it is God who works in you both to will and to do for His good pleasure." It is His perseverance with us that enables us to persevere to the end. To God be all praise and glory.

---

9. Elizabeth Cecilia Douglas Clephane, 1830–1869.

Questions

1. How should we understand Psalm 23 compared to Psalms 44 and 88, for example, as reflective of the life of faith?

2. How does the heavenly Shepherd provide for the needs of His sheep?

3. Without the Holy Spirit, John Owen said, we may as well burn our Bibles. Is Owen right? If so, why?

4. How does the Holy Spirit work with the word He inspired?

5. What weight should we give to humanly devised confessions of faith in our Christian lives?

—3—

The Heavenly Shepherd Restores His Sheep

He restores my soul.

Psalm 23 is one of the most hope-filled songs in the Psalter. More than anything else, it is a song of trustful confidence in God. David makes no pleas, no petitions, no intercessions. He simply rejoices in God's great goodness to him. Delighting in God is not a joy reserved for "elite Christians"; it is a privilege that the gospel brings to every believer. Biblical religion is natively affectional and experiential. The life of faith is rooted and grounded in God Himself, the God who is "the blessed and only Potentate, the King of kings and Lord of lords, who alone has immortality, dwelling in unapproachable light" (1 Tim. 6:15–16). It is into the fellowship of the triune God that the gospel initiates us. Yes, our minds are instructed and enriched, but our hearts no less are embraced by an everlasting love (Jer. 31:3).

Thus far we have seen an unfolding progression in the psalm. The opening words form its theme, then, step by step, David unpacks for us what it means for the Lord to be his Shepherd. Not least among the Lord's great goodness to him is "He restores my soul." There are few words more sweet to a Christian's ears than "He restores my soul." The reason why is surely obvious: we all know only too well what it is to stray from our kind and heavenly Shepherd, to defect in our hearts from His love and grace, to be seduced away from His fellowship by the fleeting pleasures of sin. But how are we precisely to understand these words? The verb David uses here, *restores*, has a range of meanings, but at its heart it means to "turn back." "He turns me back" to Himself. There are perhaps two ways to understand David.

He Refreshes My Soul

David could mean "He refreshes my soul"; that is, He restores freshness to my life. If you read verse 3 in the light of verse 2, this makes good sense, and it is wonderfully true. Are there not times in your life when you become spiritually jaded, when the gospel is not as sweet to your taste as it once was, when you find worship on the Lord's Day lacking in delight, when you just feel washed out? You understand William Cowper's words, "Where is the blessedness I knew when first I saw the Lord. Where is the soul-refreshing view of Jesus and his word."[1] Every Christian longs to be refreshed in spirit, especially during times of spiritual drought.

How, then, does the Lord refresh the lives of His sheep? He principally does so through the reading and ministry of His Word. The psalmist tells us that God's law—His teaching, His instruction—is wise, right, pure, enlightening, and righteous; it is more precious than fine gold and sweeter than honey from the honeycomb (Ps. 19:7–11).

---

1. From William Cowper's hymn "O for a Closer Walk with God" (1772).

There are times in our lives when it is a struggle, even a battle, to read God's Word. Perhaps your circumstances are all against you, disappointments have overwhelmed you, your health is precarious, or life is just hard. The devil will do all he can to persuade you to leave off reading the Bible. Perhaps you have stopped reading God's Word because it seemed to be doing nothing for you. But this is precisely when you must resolve and battle, crying out to the Lord to keep you on track. Every Christian would love every encounter with the Word of God to be immediately enriching, soul stirring, heart affecting, mind elevating. However, it is not always so. It could be that we have been prayerless or listless and not heeded the prayer of the psalmist: "Open my eyes, that I may see wondrous things from Your law" (Ps. 119:18). Or it could be that the Lord, for His own reasons, leaves us to plow a lonely furrow for a season, teaching us to live by faith and not by sight. Whatever the case, our great need is to commit to the faithful, prayerful reading of God's Word—the bread that we cannot live without, or so said our Lord Jesus Christ (Matt. 4:4)—and not forsake the assembling together of God's people (Heb. 10:25). There are few more important disciplines in the life of faith than the discipline of making the Lord's Day corporate worship a nonnegotiable priority. In His great grace, the Lord has given to His church pastors and teachers to minister His Word, and through His Word His comfort, consolation, encouragement, and rebukes to His sheep. When we absent ourselves from the fellowship of the church, we cut ourselves off from the spiritual nourishment the Lord is providing for us through His ordained servants.

Spiritual refreshment is not reserved for the public gatherings of God's people on the Lord's Day, but it is on those divinely ordained occasions that the Lord is surely most pleased to bless, strengthen, reassure, and refresh His often battle-weary saints. John Owen's assistant and then successor, David Clarkson (1622–1686), preached a sermon with the striking title "The Lord Loveth the Gates of Zion More than All the Dwellings of Jacob" (see Ps. 87:2). Clarkson shows that in both the Old and New Testaments, the public worship of God was the primary concern for believers. Luke tells us that the many thousands converted at Pentecost "continued steadfastly in the apostles' doctrine and fellowship, in the breaking of bread, and in prayers" (Acts 2:42). The verb implies committed, continual devotedness to the organized meetings of the church. Of course, the Lord graciously refreshes us in our private devotions and in family worship. But neither of these can substitute for the public worship of God, when the family together calls on the Lord and together are blessed by His presence and His Word.

There is an unhealthy individualism that greatly harms both the spiritual growth of Christians and the credible witness of the church. It is only "with all the saints" that we comprehend "what is the width and length and depth and height—to know the love of Christ which passes knowledge; that you may be filled with all the fullness of God" (Eph. 3:18–19). It is with good reason that the writer to the Hebrews urges his readers, "Let us consider one another in order to stir up love and good works, not forsaking the assembling of ourselves together, as is the manner of some, but exhorting one another, and so much the more as you see the Day approaching" (Heb. 10:24–25). These Jewish converts were being pressured to turn back from Jesus and return to Judaism. One of their great needs was to stand together, above all in the public gatherings on the Lord's Day, strengthening themselves in the fellowship of the saints as they worshiped together. Spiritual refreshment is one of the ordained blessings of corporate worship on the Lord's Day.

He Restores My Soul

It is more likely, however, that David is thinking about the Lord's grace in restoring him, a believer, back to Himself. The word *restore* has the idea of being "turned back." The Bible never wearies of reminding us that the best of Christians sin. Sometimes our sins are particularly public and shameful and disgraceful (David knew that personally). No less are we guilty of sinning and wandering from the Lord in our hearts. But the grace of God is so glorious and so counterintuitive that no matter how badly you have failed or fallen, no matter how shameful and disgraceful your sin, no matter how vile your defection from Christ, "He restores my soul." The Bible has a word for this: *grace*—unimaginable, out-of-this-world kindness and mercy. Thomas Goodwin makes a wonderful statement on what the Bible means by grace. He tells us that grace is more than mercy and love; it superadds to them: "It noteth out, not simply love, but the love of a sovereign, transcendently superior, one that may do what he will, that may wholly choose whether he will love or no.… Now God, who is an infinite sovereign, who might have chosen whether ever

He would love us or no, for him to love us, and to love us with a special love, this is grace."[2]

God is not under any obligation, within Himself, or within any man or woman, to grant us grace. His grace is His undeserved kindness to judgment-deserving sinners. This is what David himself experienced in the wake of his adultery with Bathsheba and his complicity in the murder of her husband, Uriah. David, with all his kingly and spiritual privileges, could not have sunk any lower. Yet he discovered that with God there is forgiveness (Ps. 130:4) because He is rich in mercy and full of grace.

Perhaps even more dramatically, the Lord Jesus restored Peter who three times denied Him, and with curses. I had a friend who confessed Christ and then some years later turned from Him. She wrote to all her friends telling them she had abandoned Jesus. Fifteen years later she turned up in our church. I remember her asking me, "Is there hope for someone like me?" I said to her, "There is hope for worse than you." The Lord graciously restored her, and now she is in the glory of His nearer presence.

You might be thinking, "How can God do that?" For one reason, He is who He is. When Moses pleaded with the Lord to show him His glory (Ex. 33:18), "the LORD descended in the cloud and stood with him there, and proclaimed the name of the LORD. And the LORD passed before him and proclaimed, 'The LORD, the LORD God, merciful and gracious, longsuffering, and abounding in goodness and truth, keeping

---

2. Thomas Goodwin, *An Exposition of the Second Chapter of the Epistle to the Ephesians*, in *The Works of Thomas Goodwin* (Edinburgh: James Nichol, 1861–1866; repr. Grand Rapids: Reformation Heritage Books, 2021), 2:222.

mercy for thousands, forgiving iniquity and transgression and sin, by no means clearing the guilty, visiting the iniquity of the fathers upon the children and the children's children to the third and the fourth generation'" (Ex. 34:5–7). The first thing the Lord wanted Moses to know about His glory, His "true self," was that He was "merciful and gracious, slow to anger and abounding in steadfast love." He is more than that but never less than that.

The Most Privileged of Believers Need Restoring

David's words remind us that the best of Christians fall into sin and need God's restoring mercy. Never think, far less say, "It could never happen to me." It has happened to better Christians than you and me. No Christian is invulnerable to spiritual and moral declension!

Here David leaves the pastoral imagery behind. He clearly is writing out of his personal experience. He knows only too well what it is to wander away from the Lord, like a silly sheep wandering away from the security and protection of the shepherd. Whether David writes this in the wake of his tragic and shameful adultery with Bathsheba and his complicity in her husband's murder is impossible to say. It is almost unbelievable to see just how far he, with all his privileges, strayed from his heavenly Shepherd. But every Christian is only a step away from shameful sin (read 1 Cor. 10:12). Or the context may be a less obvious defection from the Lord—a cold, creeping disinterest in spiritual things, a growing luke-warmness toward the Lord Himself. Whatever the nature and character of the defection, "He restores my soul."

Thomas Manton (1620–1677) always wrote as a pastor, and his words are a timely reminder to every Christian: "Though the pleasures of sin are short and inconsiderable, yet, because they are near at hand, they have more influence than the joys of heaven, which are future and absent…many part with the joys of Christianity for the vilest price."[3] Sin can be powerfully compelling and seductive. Satan, our great enemy, has many wiles, designs, and schemes (literally "methods"; see 2 Cor. 2:11 and Eph. 6:11). It should not surprise us that Jesus's almost last words to His disciples were "Watch and pray, lest you enter into temptation" (Matt. 26:41).

Wonderfully Kind
David's words remind us of our heavenly Shepherd's mercy and kindness. However badly sin and Satan have marred your life, He restores. This richly encouraging truth punctuates the length and breadth of the Bible. Ponder the following: "'Come now, and let us reason together,' says the LORD, 'though your sins are like scarlet, they shall be as white as snow; though they are red like crimson, they shall be as wool'" (Isa. 1:18); "I will restore to you the years the swaming locust has eaten" (Joel 2:25); "I will heal their backsliding, I will love them freely" (Hos. 14:4). The Lord is unwearying in telling us that He is kind to sinners. He holds out His hands all the day long (Rom. 10:21). He takes no pleasure in the death of the wicked (Ezek. 33:11).

---

3. Thomas Manton, *The Works of Thomas Manton* (Edinburgh: Banner of Truth, 2020), 13:332.

Many people, even many Christians, cannot believe that God is as He reveals Himself to be in His Word. John Owen, writing as a pastor, understood this aberration: "At the best, many think there is no sweetness at all in him towards us, but what is purchased at the high price of the blood of Jesus."[4] Too many Christians have the strange notion that the Lord Jesus came into the world to win for us the love of His Father. Nothing could be further from the truth. The Son of God became flesh, enduring the cross and despising its shame, not to win us the Father's love but as the revelation of His Father's love to this world (John 3:16; 1 John 4:10). The heart of the eternal One is most wonderfully kind. It is on this basis that we come back to Him to be restored to His fellowship.

Reproof and Correction

At this point a question naturally arises: How does the heavenly Shepherd restore us when we have wandered far from Him? He does so principally through His Word, read and heard, and the heart-searching ministry of the Holy Spirit. God's Word is not only "a lamp to [our] feet and a light to [our] path" (Ps. 119:105); it has been God-breathed to be "profitable for doctrine, for reproof, for correction, for instruction in righteousness, that the man of God [speaking principally if not exclusively of ministers of the word] may be complete, thoroughly equipped for every good work" (2 Tim. 3:16–17). Notice the two words *reproof* and *correction*. In His written word, the Lord confronts us with His holiness, His grace, and His love. He lays bare the thoughts and intentions of our

---

4. Owen, *Communion with God*, in *Works*, 2:32.

hearts (Heb. 4:12). As we read or hear God's Word, the Holy Spirit presses its truth into our minds and hearts. So Paul proceeds to encourage young Timothy to "Preach the word! Be ready in season and out of season. Convince, rebuke, exhort, with all longsuffering and teaching" (2 Tim. 4:2).

We are given a powerful example and illustration of this ministry in 2 Samuel 11–12. David has committed adultery with Uriah's wife, Bathsheba. In an attempt to cover up his sin, David conspires to have Uriah killed. Into this tragic and sordid affair, the prophet Nathan confronts David and speaks God's word to him, laying bare his sin and God's resolve to execute His just judgment on His errant king. The effect of Nathan's faithful ministry to David is recorded by David himself in Psalm 51, where David confesses his sin and casts himself on the Lord's mercy and steadfast love. Nathan faithfully preached God's word of truth, and to a king!

But God's corrections and rebukes are not to be left to the "professionals." Paul tells the Galatian churches that "if a man is overtaken in any trespass, you who are spiritual restore such a one in a spirit of gentleness, considering yourself lest you also be tempted. Bear one another's burdens, and so fulfill the law of Christ" (Gal. 6:1–2). We all have a family obligation to support, encourage, and, where necessary, rebuke our brothers and sisters in Christ. Faithful are the wounds of a friend. This is how our Elder Brother (Rom. 8:29) ministers to His grace-adopted siblings (see Isa. 42:3).

The hymn writer captures the sheer grace of God in His dealings with His wandering and sinful sheep:

Souls of men, why will ye scatter
Like a crowd of frightened sheep?
Foolish hearts, why will ye wander
From a love so true and deep?
Was there ever kindest shepherd
Half so gentle, half so sweet,
As the Saviour who would have us
Come and gather round his feet?

There's a wideness in God's mercy,
Like the wideness of the sea;
There's a kindness in his justice,
Which is more than liberty…
For the love of God is broader
Than the measure of man's mind;
And the heart of the eternal
Is most wonderfully kind.[5]

Cosmic Restoration

The restoration of a wandering, wayward sheep is, however, part of something bigger and grander. God's ultimate purpose is to restore all things back to Himself, to fix this broken cosmos. In his letter to the church in Ephesus, Paul tells us that God, "in the dispensation of the fullness of the times," has purposed to "gather together in one all things in Christ, both which are in heaven and which are on earth—in Him" (Eph. 1:10). Every spiritual, and physical, restoration is a harbinger or anticipation of the ultimate restoration of all things in Christ. One day there will be for Christians no more

---

5. Frederick William Faber (1814–1863). The hymn is "Souls of Men, Why Will Ye Scatter."

defections, no more wanderings, no more backslidings. Our God will make "all things new" (Rev. 21:5).

There is no greater need in the church today than a rediscovery of the extravagant, out-of-this-world grace of God. No matter how badly anyone reading this may have fallen, God is rich in mercy. Throw yourself unreservedly on His love. He promises to turn away no one who comes to Him in repentance and faith: "All that the Father gives Me will come to Me, and the one who comes to Me I will by no means cast out" (John 6:37).

Questions

1. How does the Lord restore His sheep?

2. How significant is public worship for the spiritual growth of believers?

3. In what ways can a Christian guard his or her heart from falling away?

4. What does the apostle Paul mean when he writes, "Bear one another's burdens and so fulfill the law of Christ" (Gal. 6:2)?

5. How can we abuse the great Bible truth of the grace of God (see Rom. 6:1)?

4

The Heavenly Shepherd
Leads His Sheep

He leads me in the paths of righteousness
for His name's sake.

Psalm 23 is a song of heart-delight in God. David doesn't ask his heavenly Shepherd for anything; he simply delights in the Lord and His great goodness to him. It is a song filled with joy but, as we will see, also with realism (vv. 4–5). Even when the Lord appears not to be with you, He is with you. Just as the moon is always round, so the Lord is always with His children.[1]

Many Christians, perhaps especially younger Christians, are preoccupied (even obsessed) with the "problem of guidance." They fear they will find themselves outside God's will, that they might miss out on God's best. It is good to want to be

---

1. *The Moon Is Always Round* (Greensboro, N.C.: New Growth Press, 2019) is the title of a children's book written by Jonny Gibson. It is a wonderful read. The genesis of the book goes back to the stillborn death of Jonny's infant daughter. As Jonny tried to explain to his three-year-old son that his little sister would not be coming home with them, he told him that just as the moon is always round, even when it appears not to be round, so God is always good, even when it appears He is not.

in the center of God's will (no right-thinking Christian would want anything else). But too often we are concerned about guidance in a wrong way and we become anxious, apprehensive, tentative. We can end up too much concerned about "getting it right" rather than simply living to please God.

The Promise of Guidance

The One who is responsible for guiding the sheep is the Shepherd. No sane shepherd would leave His sheep to wander around, trying to find the right way. In the life of faith, the responsibility for guiding believers is principally the Lord's. He leads and we follow. He is the Shepherd; we are His sheep. It is His responsibility to lead and it is ours to follow. Sheep are dozy and clueless. Without a shepherd to lead them, they would be in a perpetual mess. So, the Lord God Almighty has taken on Himself the responsibility to guide His sheep, His believing people, safely and purposefully. This is where the Christian's confidence about guidance ultimately lies: "He knows the way that I take" (Job 23:10).

You need to pause and understand what I am saying. I am not saying you can do your own thing—living heedless of the Lord's glory and pursuing your own selfish interests—and God will continue to guide you. He will continue to guide you, but He will guide you into His displeasure and judgment. Believers have a responsibility to follow the Lord in the paths He has set before us in His Word, paths that are well marked out, paths that only the disobedient fail to recognize.

In earlier times, there were no books written on the subject of guidance. There were, however, many books written on the subjects of God's providence and the believer's responsibility to live a life of loving obedience to the Lord (John 14:15).

The Experience of Faith

Let me dwell on this for a moment. The Christian life is natively experiential. Faith in Christ takes you into Christ, into His saving love and fellowship (1 Cor. 1:9). But the Christian life is not lived principally out of our experience of Christ; no, it is lived out of our union with Christ. Do you understand the point I am making? Jesus said, "If you love Me, keep My commandments" (John 14:15). That is a categorical statement. The reality, however, is that our love for the Savior rises and falls. There are days when our love for Him knows no bounds, but there are days when our love for Him is weak and faint (to quote William Cowper). But our obedience to Him is never to vary; it is never to be fueled by the vagaries of our love, but by the fact of our love—a love that is grounded in His prior love for us (1 John 4:19). So in the area of guidance, we are to follow the Good Shepherd, which in practice (as we will see) means keeping His commandments, both when times are good and when times are bad.

This truth, that the Lord has taken it on Himself to guide His sheep, is a wonderful comfort to Christians who long to please the Lord, who want in all their ways to honor Him. The sovereign, all-wise, kind, and purpose-filled guidance of the divine Shepherd is a promise to cherish. Throughout the Bible, guidance is never presented as a problem Christians have to solve. No, it is a promise they are to prize. I am not saying that guidance will always be straightforward. Not at all. But the Good Shepherd promises not only to lead us but also to be with us every step of the way. He is pledged in the blood of His only begotten Son to lead all His sheep safely into the glory of His nearer presence.

The Biblical Shape of Guidance

The Lord leads His flock only and always "in paths of righteousness." Good shepherds only lead their sheep in good ways; they never expose them to unnecessary dangers. For example, you can be sure that God never guides His people into disobedience. He will never lead you to follow other gods, to worship idols, to take His name in vain, to dishonor the Sabbath day, to dishonor your parents, to murder, to commit adultery, to steal, to lie or cheat, to covet what is not yours. (Did you realize I have just highlighted the Ten Commandments?) Nor will He lead you to marry an unbeliever. He will never lead you to put consequences before truth. He will not lead you to act arrogantly or proudly or selfishly. Never! He always leads His sheep "in the paths of righteousness."

But what more precisely are these "paths of righteousness"? And where do we find them? In general, the heavenly Shepherd guides us in the path of His written word, the Bible. The psalmist understood that God's Word was a lamp to his feet and a light to his path (Ps. 119:105). The apostle Paul understood that if the man or woman of God wants to "be complete, thoroughly equipped for every good work," then they must receive God's inspired (literally "God-breathed") Word as "profitable for doctrine, for reproof, for correction, for instruction in righteousness" (2 Tim. 3:16–17). In other words, "paths of righteousness" are Bible paths. The Christian life, the life of faith, is exclusively a Bible-shaped life.

It must be understood, however, that Reformed Protestants don't despise tradition. *Sola Scriptura* does not mean we pay no attention to the creeds, confessions, and catechisms of the church. To do this would be to trample on the faith and Holy Spirit insights given to our forebears throughout history. Documents such as the Apostles' Creed, the Nicene-Constantinopolitan Creed, Heidelberg Catechism, and the Westminster Confession of Faith are rich in their exposition of biblical truth and often memorable in their expressions of those truths. Nor do we despise culture. But, as Herman Bavinck so often reminded us, grace does not destroy nature; it redeems and purifies it.

Today we tragically see the visible church increasingly becoming a willing prisoner of the prevailing culture. *Sola Scriptura* is being replaced by *sola cultura*. In direct contrast to this, the believer's constant concern is what God's holy Word has to say. Isaiah put the matter simply and beautifully: "To the law and to the testimony! If they do not speak according to this word, it is because there is no light in them" (Isa. 8:20).

Obedience to the Scripture

It would be foolish, however, to think that because we read God's Word and believed its truth, we must therefore be walking in the paths of righteousness. To walk in the paths of righteousness is to live in heart obedience to the heavenly Shepherd's commands. This is what many modern Christians find so hard to believe. They hear the word *commandment* and think of legalism. But God's commands are not weights to drag you down; they are wings to help you fly. The apostle

John assures us that "His commandments are not burdensome" (1 John 5:3).

Let me ask you this question: What do you think is the purpose of the Ten Commandments? Do you think God is out to rob you of joy? Is He a heartless killjoy? Is He only happy saying no? Did you know that the New Testament describes God as the "happy" God? (In 1 Tim. 1:11, the Greek adjective *makarios* simply means "happy.") When the Lord Jesus Christ said, "I have come that they may have life, and that they may have it more abundantly" (John 10:10), He was not expressing a personal opinion; He was revealing the heart of God toward sinners.

It is your doctrine of God that will ultimately shape how you live. Once you are persuaded that He made you, is perfectly wise and good, and alone knows what is good and best for you, you will run in the path of His commandments (Ps. 119:32). He knows the folly and sin in all of our hearts, and like the best of fathers He puts hedges around us for our own good. God's commandments are the commands of a loving Father, who spared not His only Son but delivered Him up for us all. He is a Father whose goodness is unimpeachable. He is a Father who is pledged in the blood of His Son to do His children good, and nothing but good.

The Lord Our Righteousness

We need now to ask just what that will mean in daily life. In the Bible, *righteousness* has a multifaceted meaning. First, it means living "in the right way." Life is full of wrong ways, ways that will lead us to death. Proverbs tells us that "there is a way that seems right to a man, but its end is the way of death"

(Prov. 14:12). Jesus speaks of a broad way that leads to destruction and a narrow way that leads to life (Matt. 7:13–14). Your greatest need, and mine, is to know the right way, the way that leads to life and not to destruction! As you read through, for example, the Gospel of John, it becomes increasingly clear that Jesus Himself is the way of righteousness. First, He is the narrow way that leads to life: "I am the way, the truth, and the life. No one comes to the Father except through Me" (John 14:6). Only as you go to the Father through Him, the "new and living way" (Heb. 10:20), will you find acceptance with God and life—that is, fellowship with God.

This truth is beautifully pictured for us in the words of Jeremiah 23:6: "THE LORD OUR RIGHTEOUSNESS." In the gospel, God clothes us with the perfect righteousness of His Son. Paul picks up this truth in one of the Bible's most glorious, if unfathomable, verses: "He [God] made Him who knew no sin to be sin for us, that we might become the righteousness of God in Him" (2 Cor. 5:21). Jesus, His person and work, is the righteousness that unrighteous sinners are called to embrace. Christ Himself is our life (Col. 3:4). The apostle Paul understood this truth, and it captivated his life. He told the church in Philippi, "For to me, to live is Christ, and to die is gain" (Phil. 1:21).

To Live Is Christ

What is Paul actually saying in these memorable words? What does it mean to say, "For to me, to live is Christ, and to die is gain"? It is possible that Paul is saying, "It means that my whole life, all I am, is lived for Christ, His praise, His honor, the spread of His kingdom." That would be true. That is what every spiritually healthy Christian would say. But is that quite what Paul is saying here? To say that for you, "to live is Christ," is more, I think, than to say that you live your life *for* Christ. He is saying that for him Christ *is* his life. He does not merely live to serve Christ, to give his all in His service. In the Greek text there is no verb *is*: "For me to live, Christ." I recently read a quote from Martyn Lloyd-Jones that struck a deep chord with me. He was suffering a terminal illness and could no longer preach. He was asked, "Do you miss preaching?" That was a question I am sure I would have asked. He replied, "I never lived for preaching." I think Paul would have shouted a loud amen. Martyn Lloyd-Jones was a preeminent preacher, perhaps the "greatest" preacher of the twentieth century, but he did not live to preach Christ; he lived to know Christ (see Phil. 3:8–11).

It is a great privilege to serve the Lord Jesus Christ, but there is a prior and greater privilege, "that I may know Him." Any meaningful human relationship contains the same dynamic: I don't live first to serve my wife, Joan (though I love to serve her), but to love and cherish her, to be "with her." Those two little words remind us that when Jesus called His disciples, He first called them to be "with Him" (Mark 3:14). Of course, we need to understand that this "withness" gave the necessary dynamic to the ministry that Jesus entrusted to them. To love Christ is to live a life of obedience to Him (John 14:21). But what any wife or husband is seeking from their spouse is first their heart affection, their company.

Jesus Himself is the epitome of the paths of righteousness. God our Father leads us in our union with His Son. The

Lord Jesus Christ is the nourishment that sustains us as we navigate the uncertainties of this fallen world.

The Purpose of Guidance

Notice the great reason why the Lord leads us in paths of righteousness: "for His name's sake." God's name is all that He is. He is the High and Holy One who inhabits eternity. He is the King, immortal, invisible. He is the unchanging and unchangeable "I am." He is Father, Son, and Holy Spirit.

God's first concern is for the integrity, honor, and faithfulness of His own reputation. He is a righteous God and is committed to pursuing righteousness in all He does. If the Lord did not lead His flock in the paths of righteousness, He would be denying who He is. This is an antidote to our "fallen default," that my pleasure is the purpose of my life. But the purpose of the Christian's life is God's honor and praise. The first question of the Westminster Shorter Catechism put this memorably:

Q: What is the chief end of man?

A: To glorify God and enjoy him forever.

To some, it may seem self-indulgent for God to guide His people to suit Himself. The reverse is the case. God made us and knows what is best for us. He knows that our greatest good is found in knowing Him, loving Him, and following Him. In the opening chapter of *Our Reasonable Faith*, Herman Bavinck beautifully expresses this truth:

All men are really seeking after God…but they do not all seek Him in the right way, nor at the right place. They seek Him down below, and He is up above. They seek Him on the earth, and He is in heaven. They seek Him afar, and He is nearby. They seek Him in money, in property, in fame, in power, and in passion; and He is to be found in the high and holy places, and with him that is of a contrite and humble spirit (Isa. 57:15).… They seek Him and at the same time they flee Him…. In this, as Pascal so profoundly pointed out, consists the greatness and miserableness of man. He longs for truth and is false by nature. He yearns for rest and throws himself from one diversion upon another. He pants for a permanent and eternal bliss and seizes on the pleasures of the moment. He seeks for God and loses himself in the creature.[2]

Bavinck is echoing the immortal words of Augustine of Hippo in the opening paragraph of his *Confessions*: "For thou has created us for thyself, and our heart cannot be quieted till it may find repose in thee."[3] Our highest good and deepest joys are found in God. When He is honored and praised, the heart of a believer swells with delight.

When a believer is asked, "Why do you live like that?" their answer is immediate and instinctive: "To please and honor my righteous, holy, good, and gracious Father in heaven."

All God does, He does "for His name's sake," to show who He is, to show that He is holy, just, rich in mercy, kind, faithful, a hater of sin, a lover of what is good and right. More than anywhere, it is in the cross of His only begotten Son that God reveals who He is. Yes, He reveals His gracious—gloriously

---

2. Herman Bavinck, *Our Reasonable Faith* (Grand Rapids: Baker, 1956), 22–23.

3. Augustine of Hippo, *The Confessions* (Cambridge, Mass.: Harvard University Press, 2006), 3.

gracious—love; but no less does He demonstrate His righteous justice. In the Lord Jesus Christ, God placarded to the world His righteousness—the righteousness that justifies sinners through faith alone, in Christ alone (Rom. 3:22), but also the righteousness that requires that sin be justly punished. Nowhere is this more clearly expressed than by the apostle Paul in Romans 3:25–26: "whom God set forth as a propitiation by His blood, through faith, to demonstrate His righteousness, because in His forbearance God had passed over the sins that were previously committed, to demonstrate at the present time His righteousness, that He might be just and the justifier of the one who has faith in Jesus."

The paths of righteousness are those paths that reflect and explicate God's character as the righteous One.

Heart Communion

If we left matters here, we would miss a vital element in what it means for believers to walk in the paths of righteousness. Throughout its history, the church has often, very often, been diverted from the Lord's paths of righteousness. Tragically, the diversion often becomes apparent only when it is in full flower. This was perhaps the greatest tragedy of God's old covenant church. Long before God's people openly and deliberately abandoned the authority of His written Word, they had defected from Him in their hearts. Twice in Deuteronomy, God impressed on His covenant people that their physical circumcision was to be accompanied by heart circumcision (Deut. 10:16; 30:6). It is only too possible to trust in covenant privileges and not in the gracious God who gave those privileges. This is why it is imperative to understand that biblical religion is natively experiential. God looks on our hearts. He sees past our outward observance of His ways into our hearts.

I say this to make this vital point: the paths of righteousness are to be walked in heart fellowship with the heavenly Shepherd. Perhaps more than any others, the seventeenth-century English Puritans understood this.

In volume 7 of his *Collected Works*, Thomas Goodwin considers the love of Christ, "who died to make us his friends, though he could have created new ones cheaper."[4] He continues,

> Mutual communion is the soul of all true friendship… (and) friendship is most maintained and kept up by visits; and these, the more free and less occasioned by urgent business…the more friendly they are…we use to check our friends with his upbraiding, You still come when you have some business, but when will you come to see me?…. The very sight of a friend rejoiceth a man…. Personal communion with God is the end of our graces…. And as for duties, the journey's end of them is fellowship with God.[5]

The "paths of righteousness" are rich in communion with the Good Shepherd. This Shepherd not only leads His sheep; He has an intimate, personal attachment to them and love for them. In his great work *Communion with God*, John Owen understands the mutual intimacy of this fellowship. He wrote,

---

4. Goodwin, *Gospel Holiness in the Heart and Life*, in *Works*, 7:193.
5. Goodwin, *Gospel Holiness in the Heart and Life*, in *Works*, 7:197–98.

Let believers exercise their hearts abundantly unto this thing. This is choice communion with the Son Jesus Christ. Let us receive him in all his excellencies, as he bestows himself upon us;—be frequent in thoughts of faith, comparing him with other beloveds, sin, world, legal righteousness; and preferring him before them, counting them all loss and dung in comparison of him.... Let us tell him that we will be for him, and not for another: let him know it from us; he delights to hear it, yea he says, "Sweet is our voice, and our countenance is comely"; and we shall not fail in the issue of sweet refreshment with him.[6]

Owen proceeds to highlight the intended intimacy of fellowship that is held out to believers in Revelation 3:20: "Behold, I stand at the door and knock. If anyone hears My voice and opens the door, I will come in to him and dine with him, and he with Me." The "paths of righteousness" are not merely right paths; they are paths to be walked in fellowship with the heavenly Shepherd, receiving the assurances of His love and responding with heart affection to Him who first loved us.

The Christian life, the life of faith in Jesus Christ, can never be a solitary life. Even when we feel alone, we are not alone. Even "when darkness seems to veil his face,"[7] our good and gracious Shepherd is with us and by His Spirit in us.

---

6. Owen, *Communion with God*, in *Works*, 2:59.
7. Edward Mote (1797–1874), "My Hope Is Built on Nothing Less."

Questions

1. How does the heavenly Shepherd lead His sheep?

2. What Bible truths should fill our minds and hearts when we find ourselves overwhelmed by our circumstances or simply have no assurance concerning the right way to go in life?

3. Why can it be dangerous to interpret God's providence in our lives and make decisions based on our interpretation?

4. What is the ultimate purpose of God's guidance (see Rom. 8:29)?

5. What makes obedience sweet for a Christian?

The Heavenly Shepherd
Never Leaves His Sheep

*Yea, though I walk through the valley of the shadow
of death, I will fear no evil; for You are with me;
Your rod and Your staff, they comfort me.*

It is doubtful if there are more reassuring and comforting words in all the Bible for Christians. I have read these words hundreds of times at funerals of both believers and unbelievers (although no one knows for sure in what spiritual state anyone dies): of believers, to highlight their unassailable security in the face of death, "you are with me"; of unbelievers, to highlight the hope that only believers have in the face of death. Only those who have the Lord as their Shepherd can have such confidence.

However, it is difficult to know just how to understand what David writes here. Clearly, he is still thinking about the way the heavenly Shepherd leads His sheep. We saw in verse 3 that He always leads His sheep "in the paths of righteousness." But now David tells us that those paths of righteousness may lead the sheep into "the valley of the shadow of death." The Good Shepherd knows best how to lead His sheep. He is all wise, all knowing, all powerful, and all good. He knows there will be times when the good of His sheep, their everlasting good, can best be served by Him leading them through the darkest of life's valleys. The question we face is, What does David have in mind? What is this "valley of the shadow of death"?

The Dark Valleys of Life

He could mean (and the words mean this in other places), "When I am in the midst of dark and overwhelming troubles, You are with me." Sometimes the way to richer pasture leads through dark, dangerous valleys. In the Christian life, the Lord does not spare us from life's dark valleys. The Lord Jesus forewarned His disciples, "In the world you will have tribulation" (John 16:33). In Romans 8:18, Paul speaks of "the sufferings of this present time." In 2 Corinthians 11, Paul catalogs an astonishing list of troubles and trials that marked his life (vv. 23–28). He knew from his own experiences that the believing life does not protect you from trials and troubles.

I have little doubt that some, perhaps many, who are reading these words know what it is to live through times of great sadness, loss, and disappointment. Many believers experience the suffering and hostility that come from faithfulness to the Lord Jesus Christ and His gospel. In the catalog of sufferings that Paul details in 2 Corinthians 11, three words capture what it means to walk through the dark valleys of gospel faithfulness: "in deaths often" (v. 23). "In deaths often," but "You are with me."

The Lord promises that no matter how dark and difficult your trials and troubles are, He will be with you. His promise is absolute: "I will never leave you nor forsake you." So we may boldly say, "The LORD is my helper; I will not fear. What can man do to me?" (Heb. 13:5–6).

The Dark Valley of Death

However, it is more than possible David means, "When death reaches out to claim me, You are with me." There are valleys and then there is *the* valley. There is a valley we all must enter: "It is appointed for men to die once, but after this the judgment" (Heb. 9:27). Life is not endless; it has an ordained terminus. How is the Christian believer to face that final frontier? With the sure and certain confidence of the psalmist: "I will fear no evil; for You are with me." The apostle Paul elaborates on this sure and certain confidence in 1 Corinthians 15:55–57: "'O Death, where is your sting? O Hades, where is your victory?' The sting of death is sin, and the strength of sin is the law. But thanks be to God, who gives us the victory through our Lord Jesus Christ." While preparing His disciples for His imminent departure, our Lord Jesus encouraged them not to lose heart but to be comforted with the assurance that in His Father's house were many mansions and that He was going ahead to prepare a place for them (John 14:1–3). By His sin-atoning death and resurrection triumph over sin, death, and the devil, the Lord Jesus Christ has made death a pathway to life for all who rest the weight of all that they are on the grace and love of all that He is. The hymn "Our Lord Christ Hath Risen" captures this truth with pointed clarity:

> Our Lord Christ hath risen!
> The tempter is foiled;
> His legions are scattered,

His strongholds are spoiled.
O sing, alleluia! O sing, alleluia!
O sing, alleluia! be joyful and sing,
Our great foe is baffled,
Christ Jesus is King!

O Death, we defy thee!
A stronger than thou
Hath entered thy palace;
We fear thee not now!
O sing, alleluia! O sing, alleluia!
O sing, alleluia! be joyful and sing,
Death cannot affright us,
Christ Jesus is King!

Some unbelievers face death with a swagger: "Bring it on." But they only say that because they have refused to listen to God's Word. Death is not simply an inevitable natural process; "the wages of sin is death" (Rom. 6:23). Death is unnatural. It was God's judgment on sin. Death confirms your eternal destiny. Death will usher you into Christ's nearer presence or shut you out forever from the presence of the Lord. It will send you straight to heaven or cast you forever into hell. Are you ready to die?

"Not of Works Lest Anyone Should Boast"

David's unqualified assurance that he need fear no evil as he faces the valley of the shadow of death has no room for boasting. David makes no mention of his good works or even of his faith and faithfulness. David understood only too well that faith rises and falls. He understood, to his own deep shame, that faithfulness can be admirable and then lie in sinful tatters (see his awful adultery with Bathsheba and his complicity in the murder of her husband, Uriah, in 2 Samuel 11). As David contemplates the valley of the shadow of death, his sole confidence is "You are with me." The story is told of David Dickson, one of the great seventeenth-century Scottish Covenanters. As he lay dying, he was asked what he was thinking. He replied, "I am taking all my good deeds and all my bad deeds and casting them before the cross of my Saviour." Two centuries later, John "Rabbi" Duncan, one of the Free Church of Scotland's eminent professors, reflected on Dickson's confession. He said to his students, "The only difference between me and David Dickson, is that I have no good deeds to cast before my Saviour's cross." David Dickson spoke well; "Rabbi" Duncan spoke better.

The Special Comfort

There is one thing we have not yet considered: What does David mean by "Your rod and Your staff, they comfort me"? The rod was a club that was used to drive off wild animals. It was never used on the sheep but was a heavy instrument used to protect them from marauding predators. The staff was a slender pole with a little crook on the end that was used to aid the sheep. It could be hooked around the leg of a sheep to pull it from harm or be used as an instrument to direct and occasionally discipline the sheep with taps on the side of the body.

Understanding how shepherds tend their sheep helps us in understanding the character of God. When I go wandering away, He doesn't say, "There goes that stupid sheep," and then WHAM! down comes that big club! No, His attitude always is "How can I help My sheep? How can I move in to bring him back into line? How can I comfort him and supply what he needs?" God may have to discipline, but He always does it in love. He reproves, corrects, encourages, and instructs in righteousness, dealing with us firmly and gently. This is exactly what the apostle Paul tells us is the God-ordained purpose and function of Holy Scripture (2 Tim. 3:16–17).

How, then, does God use His Word to protect, rescue, comfort, and reassure His sheep? More particularly, how does God minister His comfort to His struggling and at times suffering and dying children? All of God's sheep are prone to wander, and we need our heavenly Shepherd to keep us in the way of righteousness.

The Shepherd's Presence

First, He comforts and reassures us by His presence with us: "I am with you always" (Matt. 28:20). This Shepherd never leaves His sheep. He has bound Himself to us by "the blood of the everlasting covenant" (Heb. 13:20). In Christ we are His sons and daughters; we are family (John 14:23). The Westminster Shorter Catechism captures the promised protection and care of the heavenly Shepherd for His own:

> Q. 26. How doth Christ execute the office of a king?
>
> A. Christ executeth the office of a king, in subduing us to himself, in ruling and defending us, and in restraining and conquering all his and our enemies.

The Shepherd's "rod and staff" are physical pictures of His personal, covenant-pledged commitment to be our God.

The Shepherd's Promises

Second, He comforts and reassures us by His promises to us. The apostle Peter writes of God's "exceedingly great and precious promises" (2 Peter 1:4). We could profitably spend some time simply highlighting the scope and richness of those promises. Let me mention two. The writer to the Hebrews reminds his hard-pressed readers,

> "My son, do not despise the chastening of the LORD,
> Nor be discouraged when you are rebuked by Him;
> For whom the LORD loves He chastens,
> And scourges every son whom He receives."

> If you endure chastening, God deals with you as with sons; for what son is there whom a father does not chasten? But if you are without chastening, of which all have become partakers, then you are illegitimate and not sons. Furthermore, we have had human fathers who corrected us, and we paid them respect. Shall we not much more readily be in subjection to the Father of spirits and live? For they indeed for a few days chastened us as seemed best to them, but He for our profit, that we may be partakers of His holiness. Now no chastening seems to be joyful for the present, but painful; nevertheless, afterward it yields the peaceable fruit of righteousness to those who have been trained by it. (Heb. 12:5–11)

The heavenly Shepherd loves His sheep so much that He refuses to indulge them or leave them to wander aimlessly from Him. Rather, He promises, if need be, to discipline His sheep for their good. True love is always willing to take decisive action to secure the good of the object of its love. When the Lord humbles His people, it is always "for our profit." His disciplines may well be painful, but they have a glorious goal, "that we may be partakers of His holiness."

A second precious and great promise is one that has ministered comfort and reassurance to Christians throughout the ages: "And we know that all things work together for good to those who love God, to those who are the called according to His purpose" (Rom. 8:28). Far from being an encouragement to licentious living ("God will always be there to work our sins for our good"), this promise is a comfort to believers for whom life has been a catalog of trials and sorrows—some even of their own making. The heavenly Shepherd wants His dearly loved children to know that He is sovereignly, if mysteriously, working all things for their good. There is an unfathomableness to this gospel promise. Yet Paul can write, "And we know." How can we know this? How can we be absolutely assured that God will indeed work not some things, not most things, but *all* things for our good? The answer Paul gives is breathtaking: because God has a purpose for us—a divine, eternally decreed purpose to conform us "to the image of His Son, that He might be the firstborn among many brethren" (Rom. 8:29). The heavenly Shepherd will allow nothing to come between Him and His purpose, first to conform His believing people to the likeness of His Son and ultimately to make His Son the firstborn of many brothers.

We must never forget that our salvation and sanctification are God's proximate (secondary) purpose; the glory of the Lord Jesus is His ultimate (primary) purpose. This great and good Shepherd will allow nothing and no one to deflect Him from His eternal purpose to make His Son the firstborn of many brothers. In all His shepherding, this Shepherd uses

His rod and staff to keep His sheep safe and secure, to over-rule their sins for their good and for the greater glory of His Son. Using sin sinlessly to further and perfect His eternal purpose is one of the glories of the heavenly Shepherd.

John Bunyan's *Pilgrim's Progress* is a timeless classic. As Christian and Hopeful come to the end of their pilgrimage, they find that they must still cross the River of Death before they could enter the Celestial City. Bunyan beautifully describes the scene:

> Then they asked the men if the waters were all of a depth. They said, No; yet they could not help them in that case; for, said they, you shall find it deeper or shallower as you believe in the King of the place. Then they addressed themselves to the water, and entering, Christian began to sink, and crying out to his good friend Hopeful, he said, I sink in deep waters; the billows go over my head; all his waves go over me. Selah…. Then I saw in my dream, that Christian was in a muse a while. To whom also Hopeful added these words, Be of good cheer, Jesus Christ maketh thee whole. And with that Christian brake out with a loud voice, Oh, I see him again; and he tells me, "When thou passest through the waters, I will be with thee; and through the rivers, they shall not overflow thee." Isa. 43:2. Then they both took courage, and the enemy was after that as still as a stone, until they were gone over. Christian, therefore, presently found ground to stand upon, and so it followed that the rest of the river was but shallow. Thus they got over.[1]

---

1. John Bunyan, *Pilgrim's Progress*, in *The Works of John Bunyan* (Edinburgh: Banner of Truth, 1991), 3:163–64.

Death, not space, is the final frontier. But for the Christian, death is a defeated enemy. With the apostle Paul, every Christian can cry out, "'Death is swallowed up in victory.' 'O Death, where is your sting? O Hades, where is your victory?' The sting of death is sin, and the strength of sin is the law. But thanks be to God, who gives us the victory through our Lord Jesus Christ" (1 Cor. 15:54–57). "You are with me." And so we can sing,[2]

> How firm a foundation, ye saints of the Lord,
> Is laid for your faith in His excellent Word!
> What more can He say than to you He hath said,
> To you who for refuge to Jesus have fled?
>
> Fear not, I am with thee; Oh be not dismayed,
> For I am thy God and will still give thee aid.
> I'll strengthen thee, help thee, and cause thee to stand,
> Upheld by My righteous, omnipotent hand.
>
> When through the deep waters I call thee to go,
> The rivers of sorrow shall not overflow,
> For I will be with thee, thy troubles to bless,
> And sanctify to thee thy deepest distress.
>
> When through fiery trials thy pathways shall lie,
> My grace all sufficient shall be thy supply.
> The flame shall not hurt thee; I only design
> Thy dross to consume and thy gold to refine.
>
> The soul that on Jesus hath leaned for repose,
> I will not, I will not desert to its foes.
> That soul, though all hell should endeavor to shake,
> I'll never, no never, no never forsake!

---

2. From Rippon's *Selection of Hymns*, 1787.

Questions

1. Why does God lead His precious sheep through dark valleys?

2. In what ways is the Lord with His people when they go through the "valley of the shadow of death"?

3. The great sin of God's old covenant church was covenantal presumption. They trusted in their gospel privileges and not in the God who gave them. How can this mindset make us unfit to face the valley of the shadow of death?

4. How can we be sure that "all things work together for good to those who love God" (Rom. 8:28)?

5. How does the resurrection of one man, Jesus Christ, give us unbounded assurance in the face of life's darkest trials and death itself?

6

The Heavenly Shepherd
Protects His Sheep

*You prepare a table before me in the
presence of my enemies; You anoint my
head with oil; my cup runs over.*

Psalm 23 wonderfully highlights the Christian believer's gospel privileges. It is a constant refrain in Puritan writings that too often Christians live below their privileges. We noted earlier John Owen's words: "Unacquaintedness with our mercies, our privileges, is our sin as well as our trouble." This is a problem that can afflict the best of Christians. Like Christian in *Pilgrim's Progress*, our gaze can only too easily focus on our circumstances rather than on our blood-won privileges, leaving us despondent. Martin Luther used a memorable phrase to highlight the nature of sin, *incurvatus in se*, "sin turns us in on ourselves." This is one reason why the Reformers constantly used another Latin phrase as an antidote to sin's native tendency, *extra nos*, "outside of ourselves." Just as sin would have us look in to ourselves, the gospel would have us look out to Christ.

The letter to the Hebrews was written to Jewish converts who were suffering for their faith in Jesus as God's

Messiah-Savior. As the writer begins to conclude his letter, he encourages readers to run with endurance the race that is set before them, "looking unto Jesus, the author and finisher of our faith" (Heb. 12:2). The verb *looking* actually contains the idea of "looking away to." The writer is encouraging them to look away from themselves and their circumstances to Jesus. All our gospel privileges are found "in Christ." This is David's focus throughout Psalm 23. In every verse, David fixes his thoughts on the Lord and the fountain of blessings He has lavished on His children.

As we have seen, the believer's blessings are many; however, they are shot through with holy realism. In verse 4 we read about "the valley of the shadow of death." Now we read about enemies encircling God's sheep.

Enemies, Enemies

It is often thought that at this point David leaves his pastoral shepherd/sheep picture and speaks of the pressing reality he is presently experiencing. This is possible. But it is no less possible that David is continuing to picture the heavenly Shepherd's relationship to His precious and dearly loved sheep. Sheep are prey to vicious enemies. They are helpless and hapless when enemies come calling. Simply being a sheep means you will have enemies. A sheep's life is not trouble-free, far less care-free. In David's time, wolves, even lions, were commonplace (1 Sam. 17:34). But here David speaks confidently of the divine Shepherd's protective care of His sheep. You will notice that this Shepherd not only protects His sheep from their enemies but also "prepare[s] a table" for them "in the presence of [his] enemies." How thoughtfully the Lord provides for His sheep—not only protection from their enemies but provision in the face of their enemies, not merely deliverance but soul-nourishing deliverance! As we think how we are to interpret and apply this to God's flock, His church, His "treasured possession," a number of things are obvious.

God's Flock Is Never Free of Enemies

David speaks here of "my enemies." All through his life, David was confronted by enemies. There were international enemies (Philistines, for example). There were internal enemies, such as the tragedy of Absalom's revolt (see 2 Sam. 15–19). God's church is always faced with the enmity of a fallen world that "lies under the sway of the wicked one" (1 John 5:19). This enmity has its roots in Genesis 3:15, the seed text of the whole Bible. Holy Scripture is, in one sense, an unfolding exposition of this first gospel promise. The early Christians were confronted by the hostility of the world and, behind that hostility, the consuming hatred of Satan (Eph. 6:10–12; see Acts 4:24–31, quoting Ps. 2). We see it today in the lands of the Middle East, in China, and increasingly in the once gospel-privileged nations of the United States and Great Britain. Our Lord Jesus forewarned His disciples, "In the world you will have tribulation" (John 16:33). He had earlier told them that "if the world hates you, you know that it hated Me before it hated you. If you were of the world, the world would love its own. Yet because you are not of the world, but I chose you out of the world, therefore the world hates you. Remember the word that I said to you, 'A servant is not greater than his master.' If they persecuted Me, they will also persecute you" (John 15:18–20).

Hostility and enmity are the inevitable privileges of belonging to the living God and His Son, our Lord and Savior Jesus Christ. It is because the world hates Christ that it hates anyone who confesses Him and lives to proclaim and serve Him. A Christian's wounds are his or her battle scars.

Enemies Within

The relentless hostility of this fallen world, blinded by the god of this world (2 Cor. 4:3–4), has sought to crush the Lord's church throughout its history. But the church's greatest enemy has never been the hostility of an unbelieving world; it has always been the enemy within. In His Sermon on the Mount, Jesus warned His disciples to "beware of false prophets, who come to you in sheep's clothing, but inwardly they are ravenous wolves. You will know them by their fruits" (Matt. 7:15–16). Similarly, and even more dramatically, when Paul gathered the Ephesian elders to minister to them his final farewell, he said,

> Take heed to yourselves and to all the flock, among which the Holy Spirit has made you overseers, to shepherd the church of God which He purchased with His own blood. For I know this, that after my departure savage wolves will come in among you, not sparing the flock. Also from among yourselves men will rise up, speaking perverse things, to draw away the disciples after themselves. Therefore watch, and remember that for three years I did not cease to warn everyone night and day with tears. (Acts 20:28–31)

These must be among the most sobering verses in the Bible. Paul is speaking to men whom he in all probability ordained to be undershepherds in Christ's sheepfold. Yet he anticipates that some of them will "rise up, speaking perverse things, to draw away the disciples after themselves." It is little wonder that he exhorts them to "watch" (see also 2 Tim. 3:1–5; 1 John 2:20). The best and most privileged of churches must never imagine that they are immune from such horrible defections. Watch and pray.

It is solemn to think that there was a Judas among the Twelve! However, it is even more solemn to realize there is a Judas in all of our hearts. The Lord has wonderfully justified us by the blood of His Son (Rom. 5:10), a justification that is ours by grace alone, through faith alone; but sin still remains in us to trouble us. This remaining or indwelling sin must be reckoned with, resisted, opposed, and killed. In our own strength, even with the best will in the world, we are power-less to do this. But the Holy Spirit indwells us to enable us to put this sin that remains to death: "If by the Spirit you put to death the deeds of the body, you will live. For as many as are led by the Spirit of God, these are sons of God" (Rom. 8:13–14). One of the primary marks of God's children is that they wage relentless war against the sin that remains in them to trouble them and thence bring dishonor to the Savior and His church.

The Evil of the Tongue

Chief among the enemies within our own hearts is our tongue.

> See how great a forest a little fire kindles! And the tongue is a fire, a world of iniquity. The tongue is so set among our members that it defiles the whole body, and sets on fire the course of nature; and it is set on

fire by hell. For every kind of beast and bird, of reptile
and creature of the sea, is tamed and has been tamed
by mankind. But no man can tame the tongue. It is an
unruly evil, full of deadly poison. With it we bless our
God and Father, and with it we curse men, who have
been made in the similitude of God. (James 3:5–9)

How easily our tongues can become instruments of the devil.
It is no wonder that James exhorts us to "be swift to hear,
slow to speak, slow to wrath" (James 1:19).

All of this means that we need the whole armor of God just
to stand and not become windows of access for the Evil One
to infiltrate into the life of the people of God (Eph. 6:10–18).
Enemies are everywhere.

God's Flock Is Never Short of Provision as Well as Protection

The picture David draws for us here is simply breathtaking.
Enemies are circling, the sheep are vulnerable, but "You prepare a table before me in the presence of my enemies." As
snarling, bloodthirsty enemies threaten to pounce and devour,
the heavenly Shepherd prepares a lavish feast for His precious sheep. There is almost a surrealness to the picture. This
Shepherd not only knows just how to defend and preserve His
sheep, He knows how to provide for their every need, not least
when enemies threaten.

In Psalm 78, the psalmist indicts God's covenant people
for their unbelief. Contemptuously in their rebellion they
ask, "Can God prepare a table in the wilderness?" (Ps. 78:19).
They were questioning whether God was capable of providing for them during their wilderness wanderings. It is little

wonder that the Lord Himself responds to their unbelief with anger: "The LORD heard this and was furious; so a fire was kindled against Jacob, and anger also came up against Israel, because they did not believe in God, and did not trust in His salvation" (Ps. 78:21–22). God's pledged commitment to His people, His love and loyalty, should never be questioned. He is gloriously able to provide a table of good things for His people, even in a wilderness.

How often the church throughout its history has either doubted or denied this. Paul assured the church in Philippi, "My God shall supply all your need according to His riches in glory by Christ Jesus" (Phil. 4:19). The Lord has promised that He will never fail His people in their times of need. How much better to be sitting with the Lord around "a table in the wilderness" than living in compliance and comfort in the world without Him! William Gadsby, the nineteenth-century pastor and hymn writer, captures this truth in his hymn "Immortal Honours":[1]

> My every need He richly will supply;
> Nor will His mercy ever let me die;
> In Him there dwells a treasure all divine,
> And matchless grace has made that treasure mine.

Continuing Communion with God

You don't need much imagination to think what this table is. It is a table of "good things." What nourishment does the Lord provide for His precious sheep?

---

1. William Gadsby (1773–1844), "Immortal Honours Rest on Jesus' Head."

First, and supremely, Himself. God Himself is our soul's nourishment. Jesus said, "I am the bread of life. He who comes to Me shall never hunger, and he who believes in Me shall never thirst" (John 6:35). This is the great truth pictured for the church in the Lord's Supper. The physical signs of broken bread and poured-out wine are received by faith and feasted on. We don't simply look on and admire the signs; we receive them, digest them, and confess that here is our hope before God, in the finished work of His Son, our propitiating and propitiatory Savior. He is our life (Col. 3:4).

This is why communion with God in Christ must be the heartbeat of a Christian's life. Mere attendance at the means of grace is no substitute for heart fellowship with the God of grace. This truth is one of the principal and principial notes sounded by John Owen in his classic work *Communion with God*. Owen gives us this definition of what the Bible means by communion with God: "Our communion...with God consisteth in his *communication of himself unto us, with our returnal unto him* of that which he requireth and accepteth, flowing from that union which in Jesus Christ we have with him."[2] The basis and foundation of communion with God is union with Christ. By God's grace, believers have been vitally united to the Savior, married to Him who is the Lover of our souls, our covenant King. As in all unions, there is, says Owen, a "mutual communication," a "giving and a receiving, after a most holy and spiritual manner."[3] In communion and fellowship, God gives Himself to His people, and they give to Him what He requires and accepts: love, trust, obedience,

---

2. Owen, *Communion with God*, in *Works*, 2:8–9.
3. Owen, *Communion with God*, in *Works*, 2:9.

and faithfulness. In this most glorious of all unions, where our Maker is our Husband, He looks for and longs for the returns of love.

In classical Greek, κοινωνια (communion, fellowship) was used to describe the marriage relationship, the most intimate of all human relationships. How profoundly appropriate, then, that believers, Christ's body and bride, should have κοινωνια with their Savior. κοινωνια essentially means "to participate in, to share with." John is here highlighting the highest point of Christian experience in this world. Owen picks up this thought of marital union and writes, "Now, Christ delights exceedingly in his saints: 'As the bridegroom rejoiceth over the bride, so shall thy God rejoice over thee,' Isa.lxii.5…. His heart is glad in us without sorrow. And every day whilst we live is his *wedding day*…thoughts of communion with the saints were the joy of his heart from eternity."[4]

The Lord Himself is the nourishment that supports and sustains us as we live out our lives in a fallen, hostile world, opposed relentlessly by the devil with his nefarious wiles.

Bread for Our Souls

This foundational truth is earthed in a related truth: the living Word is never to be separated from the written Word. Jesus Himself sets us a graphic example of this in His response to the devil when He was tempted in the wilderness to turn stones into bread. He replied, "It is written, 'Man shall not live by bread alone, but by every word that proceeds from the mouth of God'" (Matt. 4:4). God's Word—His

---

4. Owen, *Communion with God*, in *Works*, 2:118.

living, authoritative, and infallibly true Word—is the daily nourishment that He has graciously provided for our souls as we journey through this vale of tears. His Word, wrote the psalmist, is "a lamp to my feet and a light to my path" (Ps. 119:105). His Word is "perfect, converting the soul…sure, making wise the simple…pure, enlightening the eyes…clean, enduring forever…true and righteous altogether. [It is] more to be desired…than gold, yea, than much fine gold…. [It is] sweeter also than honey and the honeycomb. Moreover by them Your servant is warned, and in keeping them there is great reward" (Ps. 19:7–11).

How many Christians go about spiritually malnourished because they neglect reading God's Word and hearing it preached Lord's Day by Lord's Day? A Christian must be in a backslidden condition, or self-deceived, if he or she thinks they can grow in the grace and knowledge of the Lord Jesus Christ (2 Peter 3:18) without hungering after the Word of Life.

Application for Preachers

There is surely also an application for preachers: Are you rightly dividing the word of truth (2 Tim. 2:15), taking the greatest care to nourish the hungry, often desiccated souls of your congregation? Are you merely teaching brute chunks of facts, true in themselves but not feeding God's needy sheep? Preachers are not only to declare the whole counsel of God (Acts 20:27); they are to feed the Shepherd's sheep (John 21:15–17). This is no easy thing to do. It is demanding work. This is why pastors must be wary of becoming sucked into the many different aspects of church life that can consume the best of their time and energies. Men called and set apart to feed the flock must be "one thing I do" men (read Phil. 3:13), men who devote the best of their time and energies to reading, pondering, preparing, and ministering God's life-giving Word.

A Prepared Table

We should not miss that this table of good things is a lovingly and thoughtfully prepared table. Your divine Shepherd knows your every need and has promised to supply it! But notice especially that God personally does this! The Host at every service of worship, the One who prepares and dispenses the soul-nourishing food of God's truth, is God Himself. This is not to deny the importance of pastors and teachers in the life of the church. However, these ordained ministers of the Word are channels only. Paul highlights this in 1 Corinthians 3:5–7: "Who then is Paul, and who is Apollos, but ministers through whom you believed, as the Lord gave to each one? I planted, Apollos watered, but God gave the increase. So then neither he who plants is anything, nor he who waters, but God who gives the increase." The Greek text makes the apostle's words even stronger; rather than "*Who* then is Paul and Apollos," he writes, "*What* then is Paul and Apollos?" He uses the neuter pronoun to accentuate that he and Apollos are only mere instruments. God is the One who gives the increase.

When you find yourself embattled, struggling with opposition and hostility, perhaps even from onetime professing Christians, wouldn't you just settle for protection? A table filled with good things would be a glorious bonus! But God gives and gives and gives again. He gives "exceedingly abundantly above all that we ask or think, according to the power that works in us" (Eph. 3:20). So it is here: Enemies are at hand, but "You anoint my head with oil; my cup runs over."

Holy and Happy

In the Bible, oil often signifies two things. First, there is gladness. In Psalm 45:7, we read of "the oil of gladness." In Isaiah 61:2–3, we are told that when the promised Messiah comes, He will "comfort all who mourn…console those who mourn in Zion…give them beauty for ashes, the oil of joy for mourning, the garment of praise for the spirit of heaviness." God delights to bless His people with gladness of heart. When the Lord nourishes His sheep through the ministry of His Word, He desires to make them glad, to fill their hearts with joy. The gospel comes to us as a liberating power, rescuing us from misery and death and bringing us into "the glorious liberty of the children of God" (Rom. 8:21).

Too often we are guilty of juxtaposing holiness and happiness, as if the two were mutually exclusive. The truth is that the happiest people in all the world are at the same time the holiest.

We often miss the thrust of our Savior's teaching in the Beatitudes (Matt. 5:3–12). Nine times Jesus calls certain kinds of men and women blessed: "Blessed are the poor in spirit, for theirs is the kingdom of heaven. Blessed are those who mourn, for they shall be comforted. Blessed are the meek, for they shall inherit the earth. Blessed are those who hunger and thirst for righteousness, for they shall be filled." The word *blessed* simply means "happy, delightfully content." The heavenly Shepherd desires His children to be happy, and in the Beatitudes He shows us what the essence of true happiness is.

This happiness will in measure reflect our temperaments and our cultural heritage. We must never equate exuberance with gospel joy. Gospel joy may well be "inexpressible and full of glory" (1 Peter 1:8). But no less it may be solemn and deeply reflective. However, we must not relegate exuberant joy to the periphery of the believing life or imagine that the grave and solemn are more spiritual than the happy and joyful. In the gospel, the Lord Jesus has come to replace the spirit of heaviness with a garment of praise.

Spirit Anointed

Second, the physical substance of oil is also used to signify the presence and blessing of the Holy Spirit. In the Old Testament, oil was used to anoint and set apart prophets, priests, and kings for God's service. The anointing was symbolic of God's promise to give them His Spirit in order to equip them for the work He was entrusting to them. David is confessing his wonder and delight (it is hard not to see those affections embedded in his language) that the heavenly Shepherd had so enriched his life with His blessing. In the new covenant, this blessing is magnified.

In John 7:37–39, the apostle records for us Jesus's presence at the Feast of Tabernacles: "On the last day, that great day of the feast, Jesus stood and cried out, saying, 'If anyone thirsts, let him come to Me and drink. He who believes in Me, as the Scripture has said, out of his heart will flow rivers of living water.' But this He spoke concerning the Spirit, whom those believing in Him would receive; for the Holy Spirit was not yet given, because Jesus was not yet glorified." The Greek text is even more dramatic, "for the Holy Spirit was not yet." John could hardly mean that the Holy Spirit was not yet in existence. Nor could he mean that the Holy Spirit was not active under the old covenant (read Gen. 1:2; Ps. 51:11; Isa. 63:10). From the dawn of creation, the Holy Spirit was present and active, regenerating and sanctifying God's elect, equipping and enabling God's prophets, priests, and kings. But with the death, resurrection, and glorification of Christ, the Holy Spirit has come in a new way to God's elect. Jesus told His disciples that it would be better for them that He leave them and return to heaven:

> I tell you the truth. It is to your advantage that I go away; for if I do not go away, the Helper will not come to you; but if I depart, I will send Him to you. And when He has come, He will convict the world of sin, and of righteousness, and of judgment: of sin, because they do not believe in Me; of righteousness, because I go to My Father and you see Me no more; of judgment, because the ruler of this world is judged. (John 16:7–11).

In the new covenant, the Holy Spirit, as the Spirit of the sin-defeating, Satan-conquering, death-destroying Savior, has come to indwell the lives of believing sinners.

However, this does not mean that there is nothing "more" of the Holy Spirit for Christians to experience as they live out the life of faith. In Luke 11, Jesus tells His disciples, "If you then, being evil, know how to give good gifts to your children, how much more will your heavenly Father give the Holy Spirit to those who ask Him!" (v. 13). We don't receive the Holy Spirit in parcels or in proportions. But through prayer, we can experience more of the Spirit's presence and power in our lives.

An Overflowing Cup

It is little wonder that David exclaims, "my cup runs over [overflows]." This is simply glorious. No matter how hard the enemies of God and His gospel press, God is at hand to overwhelm us with His presence and blessing. He desires not simply to give you the bare minimum in order for you to survive, but to make you what you already are, "a hyperconqueror through him who loved us" (see Rom. 8:37). The picture is just wonderful—an overflowing cup, overflowing to touch others. God's blessing is never just for ourselves; it is so that we can bless others.

Because of the heavenly Shepherd's abundant protection and provision, the people we mix with should be thinking, and hopefully asking, "Why are you so joyful? How is it you are not overwhelmed by your troubles?" Our answer should be, "Because the Lord is my Shepherd."

Here, then, is the assurance of promised provision in the face of troubles and trials—lavish provision, uncontainable provision. Our Lord Jesus did not hide from would-be disciples the cost of belonging to Him, nor did He hide from them the glorious, heavenly provisions that He promises to His own. Jesus's words in Luke 12:32, "Do not fear, little flock, for it is your Father's good pleasure to give you the kingdom," have long embedded themselves in my mind and heart. In some places in this world, God's people are a little flock, marginalized, despised, persecuted. But they have the Savior's promise that it is their heavenly Father's good pleasure to give them His kingdom. Surely our hearts can only respond with Moses and the children of Israel, "Who is like You, O LORD, among the gods? Who is like You, glorious in holiness, fearful in praises, doing wonders?" (Ex. 15:11).

Questions

1. How does the heavenly Shepherd protect His sheep?

2. Why do God's sheep have enemies?

3. How are we to confront the enemy that yet remains within us to trouble and humble us?

4. How does the Lord prepare tables in the wilderness for His beleaguered sheep?

5. What does it mean to have communion with God?

7

The Heavenly Shepherd
Leads His Sheep Safely Home

Surely goodness and mercy shall follow me
all the days of my life; and I will dwell
in the house of the LORD forever.

When I ministered in Cambridge, someone in the congregation asked me why I thought this psalm is the best known and possibly best loved of all the Psalms. At the time I wasn't quite sure how to answer. The psalm is brief and memorable. It is evocative, with imagery and language that are vivid and pictorial. The Scottish tune Crimond and the Scottish translation have been taken to every corner of our planet. However, on reflection there is really only one reason why this psalm is so indelibly etched on the minds and hearts of Christian believers: it wonderfully captures the essence of the believing life, "The Lord is my Shepherd." David is confessing the fundamental truth that shaped and directed his life. He is acknowledging that "I am His and He is mine." This is the intimate relationship that God graciously bestows on everyone who comes to Him through His Son. When you rest the weight of all that you are on the finished work of Christ, trusting in the efficacy of His shed blood to atone for your sin, God brings you into His family; you become a son, a daughter, of the living God. Horatius Bonar expressed this truth so well:

> Upon a Life I have not lived,
> Upon a Death I did not die,
> Another's Life; Another's Death,
> I stake my whole eternity.[1]

A Psalm of Faith

David wrote this psalm as a man of faith. He had come to rest the weight of all that he was on the grace and love of the Lord. The evidence that we truly are men and women of faith is not that we have a testimony we can look back to but that we are presently trusting alone in the finished sin-atoning work of our only hope and Savior, Jesus Christ.

In the previous psalm, David confessed, "You are He who took Me out of the womb; You made Me trust while on My mother's breasts. I was cast upon You from birth. From My mother's womb You have been My God" (Ps. 22:9–10). Like John the Baptist (see Luke 1:15), the Lord appears to have regenerated David while yet in his mother's womb. We must ever be wary of equating a true conversion with having a dramatic testimony. The Lord is sovereign in how He is pleased to save. Jesus told Nicodemus, "The wind blows where it wishes, and you hear the sound of it, but cannot tell where it comes from and where it goes. So is everyone who is born of the Spirit" (John 3:8).

---

1. Horatius Bonar (1808–1889), from the hymn "On Merit Not My Own I Stand."

Stepping Back

Perhaps for a moment it would be good and right to step back from the psalm. What David writes here stands in stark, dramatic contrast to how the Bible describes the human race in its natural state. By nature we all are "dead in trespasses and sins" (Eph. 2:1). No one is born into this world untainted. The Bible's assessment of every single one of us is damning: "All we like sheep have gone astray; we have turned, every one, to his own way" (Isa. 53:6). Far from being compliant, doting, obedient sheep, we are rebel sheep, self-willed sheep, natively disobedient sheep. And such we would have remained, and died in our state of rebellion, if the Lord God had not had mercy on us. He Himself, and no other, found a way to rescue us from our disobedience and self-willed wandering. He found a way to subdue our proud, sinful hearts and make us His loving, praising, obedient sheep. A few moments ago I quoted the first half of Isaiah 53:6; now read the rest of the verse: "And the LORD has laid on Him the iniquity of us all." The Welsh hymn writer William Rees beautifully expressed the grace and wonder of this great transaction:

> Here is love vast as the ocean,
> Loving-kindness as the flood,
> When the Prince of Life, our ransom,
> Shed for us His precious blood.
> Who His love will not remember?
> Who can cease to sing His praise?
> He can never be forgotten
> Throughout heav'n's eternal days.
>
> On the Mount of Crucifixion,
> Fountains opened deep and wide;

> Through the flood-gates of God's mercy
> Flowed a vast and gracious tide.
> Grace and love like mighty rivers
> Poured incessant from above;
> Heaven's peace and perfect justice
> Kissed a guilty world in love.[2]

This is what the Good Shepherd, Jesus Christ, came to accomplish in the fullness of time (Gal. 4:4–5).

All of this is the subtext of Psalm 23. You will never begin to understand the psalm until you begin to understand the salvation that caused King David to write it, or better, understand the Savior who is Himself the salvation of everyone who puts their trust and hope alone in Him alone.

In verse 5 David wrote glowingly of a feast of overflowing abundance. But the believer's ultimate prospect is better than a feast! The Lord's Table wonderfully reaffirms the Lord's covenant with His believing people, but it is not an end in itself. One day we will no longer need signs and seals. One day we shall see His face. Every Christian is heading home.

The psalm concludes with a double affirmation.

The Divine Pursuit

"Surely goodness and mercy shall follow me all the days of my life." It is probable that it should be translated "have pursued me." It is not just that the Lord's goodness and mercy have followed His precious sheep at a distance. The picture is more dynamic. God's goodness and mercy have actively pursued His sheep all their days. This is an affirmation of faith.

---

2. William Rees (1802–1883), "Here Is Love Vast as the Ocean."

If David had judged his life by what his eyes alone could see, would he have said this? Goliath! Saul! Bathsheba! Absalom! David is possibly looking back over his life, and this is his testimony: "The Lord has only ever dealt with me in goodness and covenant love."

One of a parent's greatest sins is to indulge their children's whims and notions. Too many parents hold back from "tough love": saying no, removing privileges, administering appropriate (but gentle) corporal punishment. The Bible reminds us that "whom the LORD loves He chastens, and scourges every son whom He receives" (Heb. 12:6).

There will be times in your life when the Lord will express His goodness and love to you by bringing you into "deep waters," by allowing you to experience disappointment, by withholding some great longing from you. What will you say then? Our calling in this life is to live by faith and not by sight (2 Cor. 5:7). William Cowper wrote many wonderful hymns. He experienced periods of deep darkness in his life, and it was out of those times of deep darkness that he wrote possibly his most famous hymn, "God Moves in a Mysterious Way." Some lines in the hymn are memorable:

> God moves in a mysterious way
> His wonders to perform.
> He plants his footsteps in the sea
> And rides upon the storm.
>
> You fearful saints, fresh courage take;
> The clouds you so much dread
> Are big with mercy and shall break
> In blessings on your head.

Judge not the Lord by feeble sense,
But trust him for his grace;
Behind a frowning providence
He hides a smiling face.

His purposes will ripen fast,
Unfolding ev'ry hour.
The bud may have a bitter taste,
But sweet will be the flow'r.

Blind unbelief is sure to err
And scan his work in vain.
God is his own interpreter,
And he will make it plain.[3]

Judge not the Lord by feeble sense. In the life of faith, you must learn to take every perplexing providence to the truth of Romans 8:32: "He who did not spare His own Son, but delivered Him up for us all, how shall He not with Him also freely give us all things?" Paul is arguing from the greater to the lesser: "If God gave His only begotten Son to be for you a sin-atoning sacrifice, do you think He would withhold any lesser gift from you?"

Because He is your Shepherd, your selfless, self-sacrificing Lord and Savior, you can trust Him, even when you cannot understand Him.

Full Assurance

David's confidence in the Lord is unqualified. He says "Surely," without any doubt, goodness and mercy have followed him

---

3. William Cowper (1731–1800), "God Moves in a Mysterious Way."

all the days of his life. The life of faith is not tentative. There is such a thing as "full assurance of faith" (Heb. 10:22).

At the Reformation, the Roman Church was adamantly opposed to the Reformers teaching on assurance. Robert Bellarmine (1542–1621), the greatest of the post-Reformation Roman theologians, maintained that the Protestant doctrine of assurance was "a prime error of the heretics." In its theological response to the teachings of the Reformation, the Council of Trent (1545–1563) maintained that a "believer's assurance of the pardon of his sins is a vain and ungodly confidence." More pointedly, the council declared in canon 16 on justification, "If any one saith, that he will for certain, of an absolute and infallible certainty, have that great gift of perseverance unto the end,—unless he have learned this by special revelation; let him be anathema."[4]

According to the Church of Rome, a few especially holy men and women, through special revelation, may attain to assurance of salvation, but they are the exception and certainly not the rule. It is not hard to understand why Rome is so opposed to the doctrine of Christian assurance: If "ordinary" Christians can, and should, be assured of their salvation, what need do they have of the church's priestly, sacramental mediation?

For Protestants, the controversy with the Church of Rome over assurance was at heart a controversy over its failure to understand the nature of the Trinity, especially the grace of the Father's love, the perfection of the Son's atonement, and the sealing of the Holy Spirit's indwelling presence. Rather

---

4. Council of Trent, session 6, canon 16. See http://traditionalcatholic.net /Tradition/Council/Trent/Sixth_Session,_Canons.html.

than leave His believing children uncertain of His love and uncertain of the perfect efficacy of the Savior's atonement, the Bible assures us that God, being the good God He is, wants His children to live in the joy and assurance of His love and His Son's "It is finished" (John 19:30).

It needs to be said, however, that many Christians, for diverse reasons, struggle with doubts and fears. The Westminster Confession of Faith has a most helpful and thoughtful chapter devoted to the subject of the believer's assurance:

> This infallible assurance doth not so belong to the essence of faith, but that a true believer may wait long, and conflict with many difficulties before he be partaker of it: yet, being enabled by the Spirit to know the things which are freely given him of God, he may without extraordinary revelation, in the right use of ordinary means, attain thereunto. And therefore it is the duty of everyone to give all diligence to make his calling and election sure; that thereby his heart may be enlarged in peace and joy in the Holy Ghost, in love and thankfulness to God, and in strength and cheerfulness in the duties of obedience, the proper fruits of this assurance: so far is it from inclining men to looseness.[5]

Full assurance is not the preserve of the especially godly. The good and gracious Shepherd does not want His children to live in a twilight world of uncertainty concerning His love for them and their trust and hope in Him.

---

5. Westminster Confession of Faith 18.3.

God Himself Is Our "Goodness"

Our English word *God* is from the old Anglo-Saxon term meaning "The Good." God Himself is the goodness that follows and pursues us. In the gospel God gives you Himself. He is your highest good. In Christ, God Himself is our "wisdom...righteousness and sanctification and redemption" (1 Cor. 1:30). We must learn never to separate the blessings of the gospel from the person of the Savior.

Covenant Love

Mercy is literally "covenant love" (*hesed*), pledged love, undying, blood-sealed love. This is your portion if you are one of the heavenly Shepherd's sheep. He pursues you, hunts you down, with His covenant love. David is telling us that he is "loved with everlasting love, led by grace that love to know."[6] God's love is not given to the deserving (there are none) but to the undeserving, even the hell deserving. If God were not a gracious God, no one would be loved; all of us would be lost.

David adds, "all the days of my life." God's commitment to love His sheep is forever. His commitment to us does not rise and fall depending on our commitment to Him. This is the bedrock of the Christian's assurance: not my frail hold of Him but rather His mighty grasp of me. Too often in our quest for full assurance we look into ourselves to find marks of grace. Our great need, as we have seen, is to do what the Reformers always urged their congregations to do: look away (*extra nos*) to Jesus.

---

6. George Wade Robinson (1838–1877), "Loved with Everlasting Love."

The House of the Lord

The conclusion of the psalm is no anticlimax—far from it. David's assurance transcends his present circumstances and looks forward to his eternal hope. It is no vague and uncertain hope: "and I shall dwell in the house of the LORD forever," literally "for length of days."

There is little doubt what David is saying: the day will come when God's goodness and mercy will no longer pursue him but will fully and forever embrace him. "Length of days" is not in itself an expression for eternity; but since the logic of God's covenant commitment to His sheep allows no ending, we can safely understand these words to mean that He will be forever, unendingly, in the nearer presence of the Lord.

This was one of Jesus's last promises to His disciples: "Let not your heart be troubled; you believe in God, believe also in Me. In My Father's house are many mansions; if it were not so, I would have told you. I go to prepare a place for you. And if I go and prepare a place for you, I will come again and receive you to Myself; that where I am, there you may be also" (John 14:1–3). This is the Christian hope: not that life will go on and on and on but that "we shall always be with the Lord" (1 Thess. 4:17).

The apostle Paul expounded this glorious truth memorably in his letter to the Romans: "For I am persuaded that neither death nor life, nor angels nor principalities nor powers, nor things present nor things to come, nor height nor depth, nor any other created thing, shall be able to separate us from the love of God which is in Christ Jesus our Lord" (Rom. 8:38–39).

The Christian believer has a "living hope through the resurrection of Jesus Christ from the dead" (1 Peter 1:3). All people have hopes, but not everyone has a living, death-defying, death-defeating eternal hope.

As we close, go back with me to what I said at the beginning of this little book. How is it possible that a man like David—a man who committed adultery and who was complicit in the murder of the woman's husband—could have the confidence to say, "Surely goodness and mercy shall follow me all the days of my life; and I will dwell in the house of the LORD forever" (v. 6)? Only for one reason: God is "rich in mercy" (Eph. 2:4). This is the only place in the Bible where we are told that God is rich in anything. As the Westminster Shorter Catechism reminds us, "God is a Spirit, infinite, eternal, and unchangeable, in his being, wisdom, power, holiness, justice, goodness, and truth." This is a beautiful and rich statement. But we must learn to parse it according to the Bible's own hermeneutic—that is, in the light of what God says about Himself. As we noted earlier, no passage more reveals who God is than His own self-disclosure to Moses in Exodus 34:6–7: "And the LORD passed before him and proclaimed, 'The LORD, the LORD God, merciful and gracious, longsuffering, and abounding in goodness and truth, keeping mercy for thousands, forgiving iniquity and transgression and sin, by no means clearing the guilty, visiting the iniquity of the fathers upon the children and the children's children to the third and the fourth generation.'" Note where the Lord begins His revelation—"merciful and gracious." He is more than this, but this is where God would have us begin our thinking about Him.

In the life, death, and resurrection of His own Son, God found a way to express that mercy and grace in His justification of the ungodly (see 2 Cor. 5:21). Octavius Winslow expressed this glorious truth memorably: "Who delivered up Jesus to die? Not the Jews for envy. Not Judas for money. Not Pilate for fear. But the Father for love." Truly, here is "love vast as the ocean."

Questions

1. Why can Christians be sure that the Lord will lead them safely home?

2. What is faith? What is faith's fundamental distinguishing mark?

3. How are we to understand goodness and mercy when life is hard and the devil is seeking to dismantle our faith?

4. Why is the cross of our Lord Jesus Christ the believer's ultimate assurance?

5. Why is the grace of God—or better—the God of grace, so scandalous to this world?

Soli Deo Gloria